עמותת הורים
Aseh
Chayil
באפרתה
Parents' Association

Talk of the Table

KOSHER COOKBOOK

Recipes Gathered by
the Parents' Association
of the Aseh Chayil School
Efrat, Israel

With great honor we
dedicate our cookbook
to a true hero:

Yosef Goodman
(an Aseh Chayil graduate)

*His courage and dedication
to the State of Israel will never
be forgotten.*

Psalms 137

אם אשכחך ירושלים
תשכח ימיני.
תהלים קל"ז

ISBN 965-7108-88-8

Urim Publications
P.O.Box 52287
Jerusalem 91521 Israel

Lambda Publishers Inc.,
3709 13th Avenue Brooklyn
New York 11218 USA

Tel: 718-972-5449 Fax: 718-972-6307

www.UrimPublications.com

Cover Photo: Rebecca Kowalsky
Graphic Design: Zahava Bogner

I would like to take this opportunity to thank the members of the Parents' Association – Amutat Chayil B'Efrata – for all of their efforts toward enhancing the school's educational environment in so many areas. It is due to the successful partnership between the parent body and the school administration that we are able to progress on so many important fronts. Ultimately, of course, the direct beneficiaries of all of these activities are our children; we are indeed fortunate to be blessed with parents who value the advancement of their children and who are willing to invest time and effort into their development.

Allow me to offer you a parable from the realm of cooking:

THREE POTS

The chef's daughter complained to her father about her difficulty in dealing with life's problems. The chef brought her into his kitchen and showed her three pots of boiling water.

In the first pot, he put carrots.

In the second pot, he placed an egg.

In the third pot, he poured ground coffee.

After a while, the cook pulled the carrot from the pot and put in on a plate, fished the egg from the boiling water and placed it in a bowl, filtered the coffee and poured it into a mug.

He looked at his daughter and said: "What do you see, my dear?"

The daughter approached the table and examined the products.

The carrot was soft and mushy.

The egg looked the same, but when she peeled away the skin, it was hard.

The coffee exuded a terrific smell — and its taste was delicious.

"Such are people," explained the chef. "Different people deal with the same challenge in different ways. All three of these foods were immersed into boiling water. But all three reacted differently."

He continued. "The carrot began in solid form, but it became very sensitive and vulnerable. The egg entered the water in a fragile state, full of liquid and surrounded by a thin shell, but the boiling water hardened it. And the ground coffee turned into something even more special than it was to begin with!"

Then the chef asked his daughter, "Which of these are you like? When problems knock at your door, how do you react? Like a carrot, who appears hard but loses its strength under stress? As an egg, whose gentle heart hardens after being fired, divorced or experiencing the death of a loved one... who appears the same on the outside, but whose heart and soul have become irreversibly tough? Or do you react to challenges like the ground coffee, making the absolute best of painful situations?"

People are different, and their reactions to difficult situations are different. There are those who appear strong, but who become helpless during times of trouble. There are others, seemingly gentle, who in times of crisis become hard and inflexible. And then there are those with resourcefulness and optimism who make lemonade when life offers lemons.

As parents and teachers, we need to really know the children who stand before us, to evaluate the way in which they deal with life, so that we can help them in their times of need. We must also impart to our children that in order to be like ground coffee, which achieves its fullest potential when the water boils at its hottest, we must remember that everything that happens in life has a reason... we must only discover what it is and learn from it. There is no limitation in life that can't ultimately be transformed into an advantage.

We at Aseh Chayil Elementary School believe that with professionalism, patience and love we can direct each child and bring out the best inside of him or her. With our continued joint efforts with the parent body we will, G-d willing, successfully nurture our children into successful young adults.

Miriam Weingrover
Principal

"The directive of Life is the give-and-take; this is how the world was created, that each person should both influence and receive. And he who does not possess both forces as one is like a barren tree." (R. Isaac Mezichtov)

The cookbook project, the work of volunteers in its entirety, is one of the many projects under the umbrella of the Amutat Horim – the Parents' Association. The success of the cookbook sales will help enable us to continue our activities on behalf of our children's education and successful future.

I want to acknowledge all those who contributed their delicious recipes to the book; the very special committee chairs and volunteers who devoted countless hours to organizing, editing, translating, converting and proofing; the parents who somehow completed the graphic layout, printing and binding on a shoestring budget; and of course I would like to thank you – you, who purchased this book for the benefit of our children.

It is my hope that our children, the school administration and its teachers, and all of Aseh Chayil's friends and supporters will continue to go from strength to strength, and that we will merit to persist in our pursuit of excellence in education.

B'vracha,

Avituv Zalkin
Chairman, Amutat Horim "Chayil B'Efrata"
Aseh Chayil Parents' Association

Tomer Danziger
Administrator, Amutat Horim "Chayil B'Efrata"
Aseh Chayil Parents' Association

The Parents' Association at the Aseh Chayil School would like to thank and acknowledge the following individuals and businesses whose donations made the publication of this book possible. Thank you for supporting our children – your generosity is providing meaningful enrichment programs.

500 NIS Donors

Judo Efrat,
  Yehudit Sidikman

Municipality of Efrat,
  Department of Education

250 NIS Donors

Dr. Shlomit Bach, DMD

Alan Cohl, Architect,
  Interior Design

Galgalei Etzion

Zvi Pakter, Construction &
  Renovation work

Supermarket Ish Hakiryah Efrat

Telesolar

Simcha Wachtel, Computer
  Services

David Zeller, Singer, Teacher,
  Writer in Jewish Spirituality

Hannah Sara Zeller,
  Torah Yoga & Jewish Art

180 NIS Donors

Alei Hate'ena

Dr. Avi Auerbach,
  Ophthalmology, Medical
  & Surgical

Shellie Ben-David, Certified
  Infant Massage Instructor
  & Reflexologist

Allegra Cohen, Cosmetician

Efrat Medical Center

Efrat Pharm

Itzik's Barber Shop

Dr. Karen Lawner-Gold

Yehuda Levy

Doug May, Plumbing

Sima H. Navon, Healing
  & Massage Therapy

Judy Stern, English lessons

Dr. Roy Stern, Pediatrician

Shifon Bakery

Amihud Shragai, Law Office

Super Patit Efrat

Yablochnik

Esther Zerbib, Hair & Beauty
  Salon for Women & Children

100 NIS Donors

Aluma Natural Health Food

Cafe B'rosh Tov

Chai-BaBait

Duvdevan Fashions

Etzion Judaica Center

Evergreen, Ben Ami Menzin

Achi Greenfeld, Construction
  & Repairs

Gush Phon, Jill Kuchar

Hili Fashion Boutique

Images of Efrat

Kal-Li

Lea'l'eh, Childrens' Clothing

Matemim Efrat Catering
  (Joni Liwerant)

Mintzer Books & Judaica

Miriam Realty

Na'alei Hadekel

OrliPrint Ltd.

Pizzeria Efrat, Mordechai
  & Ann Goodman

Pri-Li

Remote Radiology International

Shelley's Fashion Boutique

Silvi Hair Salon & Bridal Dresses

The Smile Health Center,
  Dr. Y. Kowalsky, Dr. N. Nevies,
  Dr. Z. Nevies

Tartufo Italian Ice Cream

Yismut, Office Services

TABLE OF CONTENTS

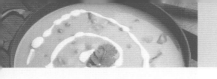

ASPARAGUS SOUP

Naama Bach

Sauté onion in butter until soft. Add asparagus.
Stir gently. Sprinkle in flour and stir. Gradually
add milk and water. Bring to boil while stirring.
Add soup powder, parsley, and sour cream.
Simmer 15 minutes, stirring occasionally.

INGREDIENTS

1 onion, chopped

2 Tbsp butter

200g (7 oz) canned
asparagus, drained
& cut

1 Tbsp flour

2 cups water

2 Tbsp mushroom
soup powder

3 sprigs parsley,
chopped

salt, pepper

1 cup sour cream

BEAN SOUP (PARO)

Ro'i Elizur

Heat oil in a large pot. Add onion. Add all ingredients
except for seasoning. Bring to boil, cook 1 1/2-3 hours.
Take care not to let it burn. Add water as needed.

INGREDIENTS

1/4 cup olive oil

1 large onion,
chopped

3 large cloves garlic

4 large tomatoes,
chopped

2 carrots, diced

2 celery stalks,
chopped

6 cups stock

salt, pepper,

4 sage leaves,
chopped

a few leaves of
rosemary

300g (10.5 oz) pearl
barley, soaked
overnight

300g (10.5 oz) wheat
berries

300g (10.5 oz) beans,
white or red

BROCCOLI SOUP

Dvir Infeld

Sauté onion in butter. Divide broccoli into florets and add to onion. Sauté for 10 minutes. Add water, flour, and seasoning. Cook about 1/2 hour. Blend, add milk, and bring to boil. Serve with croutons.

INGREDIENTS

2 large onions, chopped

1 large broccoli, cut in florets

100g (1/2 cup) butter

8 cups water

2 Tbsp soup powder

salt, pepper

flour

2 cups milk

croutons

CARROT SOUP

Gabi Spitzer

Sauté onions in oil. Add carrots and potato. Fill pot with water. Bring to boil and then add soup powder. Simmer for 1 hour. Add dill and cook 10 more minutes. Blend until smooth.

INGREDIENTS

2 onions, chopped

1 Tbsp oil

1 k (2 lbs) carrots, cut in chunks

1 potato, chopped

2 Tbsp soup powder

dill, to taste

CREAMED CORN SOUP

Shachar Has

Cook corn in a large pot. Add milk, potato, red pepper (reserve some pepper for garnishing). Cook on medium heat for 20 minutes. Blend half the soup and return to pot. Stir and cook 10 minutes until soup boils. Turn off stove, add cream, and garnish with pepper or green onion.

INGREDIENTS

400g (14 oz) corn

90g (1/2 cup) butter

2 medium potatoes, chopped

1 red pepper, chopped

1 cup water

2 cups milk

1 cup whipping creamor sour cream

1 tsp salt

pinch pepper

INGREDIENTS

4 large onions, finely chopped

4g (8 lb) sweet potato, diced

4 carrots, diced

parve chicken soup powder

white wine

nutmeg

salt

pepper

4 cups milk

1 cup cream

CREAM OF SWEET POTATO SOUP

B'rosh Tov Café | Efrat | 02 993 1693

Sauté onion in oil until golden. Add sweet potato and carrot. Continue stirring on the flame until the vegetables are soft. Add water, bring to boil and season. Continue cooking on a small flame for 1 1/2 hours. Blend the soup, adding water if too thick. Add milk, cook for 5 minutes, then stir in the cream and remove from the flame.

INGREDIENTS

1 cucumber

3-4 ripe tomatoes

4 cloves of garlic

1 green pepper

1 onion

1/3 cup oil

1/4 cup vinegar

1 1/2 liter (3 pints) tomato juice

JEREMY'S TEXAS GAZPACHO

Jeremy Brody | Houston, Texas

Puree vegetables in food processor. Add oil and vinegar to food processor. Pour in tomato juice and mix together. Serve cold.

HARIRA ("BALAGAN") SOUP

Perach Luke | Morocco

Put the vegetables, chickpeas, and lentils into a pressure cooker. Add water to cover, oil, turmeric, salt and pepper, soup powder (if desired), and cook for 20 minutes. Remove from flame and open pot when cool. Pour soup into regular pot and add water to desired consistency. Bring to boil in uncovered pot and then add lemon juice and noodles. Cook for a few minutes while stirring. The soup may be thickened by slowly adding 2 tablespoons of flour dissolved in half a cup of cold water.

INGREDIENTS

1 cup chickpeas, soaked overnight

1/2 cup green lentils

1 large carrot, diced

1 large potato, diced

3-4 celery stalks, with leaves, diced

1 ripe tomato, peeled

150g (5 oz) pumpkin, diced

1 onion, diced

2 Tbsp oil

turmeric

chicken soup powder, optional

juice of 1 large lemon

1/2 cup thin noodles

LENTIL SOUP

Noam Baer

Sauté onion in oil for 5 minutes. Add garlic, and sauté 2 more minutes. Add the rest of the ingredients and add water to cover. Cook on a low flame in a pressure cooker. Release steam after 30 minutes.

INGREDIENTS

500g (1 lb) lentils

2 large onions, finely chopped

2 Tbsp oil

3-4 cloves garlic, minced

4 Tbsp tomato puree

2 Tbsp chicken soup powder

sweet paprika

pepper, salt

5

DOUGH FOR DUMPLINGS

1 cup bulgur (tabuleh)

2/3g (23 oz) semolina

water

FILLING

1 large onion, chopped

1/2g (1 lb) chopped meat

ground parsley

salt

black pepper

baharat (allspice) for kuba

SOUP

1 large onion, chopped

3 carrots, cut in chunks

2 squash, cut in chunks

1 turnip, cut in chunks

3 stalks of celery, cut in chunks

boiling water

280g (10 oz) tomato puree

salt

black pepper

pinch of citric acid

KUBA SOUP

Hannah Ido   Iraq

DOUGH FOR DUMPLINGS

Place bulgur in bowl and add enough water to cover. Soak bulgur for 10 minutes until water is absorbed. Add semolina and mix well with fingers. Add a cup of water and knead until dough is smooth. Let stand for 15 minutes. If the dough becomes hard, add a little more water and knead again. The dough should be soft but not sticky. This is a matter of experience, and improves with time!

FILLING FOR DUMPLINGS

Fry onion until brown. Add meat, stirring continuously with fork to prevent lumps. Fry until brown and dry. Add parsley and spices.

DUMPLING ASSEMBLY

Roll a spoonful of dough into a ball. Use slightly wet hands but beware of making the dough sticky. Use your thumb to make an indentation in the ball. Fill it with 1-2 tsp of meat filling. Seal the ball and make sure there are no holes.

SOUP

Fry onion until brown and add large chunks of vegetables. Sauté for 5 minutes. Fill the pot with boiling water to 2/3 of its height. Add tomato puree and spices to taste. Bring to boil and simmer for 20 minutes. Bring the soup to boil again, and drop the balls in. Stir so that they don't stick to each other, but be careful not to break the balls open. Simmer for 20 minutes after the last ball was put in.

MOROCCAN VEGETABLE SOUP

Joy Epstein

Melt margarine in large pot. Add carrots, rutabaga, onions, prunes, turmeric, cinnamon, salt, ginger, and pepper. Cover and simmer for 10 minutes, stirring occasionally. Stir in flour and mix well. Stir in cabbage, stock, chickpeas, and tomatoes. Bring to boil. Reduce heat, cover and simmer 30-45 minutes. Serve over couscous. Delicious!

INGREDIENTS

- 4 carrots, cut in chunks
- 1/2 rutabaga (use turnip if unavailable), cut in chunks
- 3 onions, cut in chunks
- 1/2 small cabbage, cut in chunks
- 2 Tbsp margarine or oil
- 1/2 cup pitted prunes
- 1/2 tsp turmeric
- 1/2 tsp salt
- 1/2 tsp cinnamon
- 1/4 tsp ginger
- 1/4 tsp pepper
- 2 Tbsp flour
- 2 cups vegetable stock
- 1 can chickpeas, drained
- 1 can crushed tomatoes

MUSHROOM AND WILD RICE SOUP

Neria Baum

Sauté onion in oil. Add mushrooms, then rice and water. Bring to boil, reduce heat and simmer for 30 minutes. Add seasoning and soy sauce. If milk is desired, add at the end.

INGREDIENTS

- 1 onion, chopped
- 1 tsp oil
- 1 can sliced mushrooms
- 1 cup wild rice
- 8 cups water
- pinch pepper
- 1 Tbsp soy sauce
- 1 tsp salt
- 1 cup milk (optional)

ONION SOUP

Assaf Zeligman

Heat oil or margarine in pot, add sliced onions. Brown while stirring. Add water and soup powder. Add the wine, season, and cook until done.

INGREDIENTS

6 large onions, sliced into rings

oil or margarine

2 Tbsp onion soup powder

6 cups water

1/2 cup dry white wine

salt

white pepper

ORANGE SOUP

Luigi's Italian Restaurant | Jerusalem
02 623 2524

Sprinkle the pumpkin, sweet potatoes, and carrots with the sugar, salt, and oil. Bake in a 200C (400F) oven for 1 hour. Put the baked vegetables in a pot and just cover with water. Boil for 5 minutes, then cool and blend in blender. Add onion and celery. Continue blending until well blended. Return the mixture to the pot and bring to a boil. The mixture should not be too thick.
Add water if necessary. Add salt to taste, freshly ground nutmeg and chives. Bring to boil again.
Add 2 cups milk and 1 cup cream. The soup should be a yellow to orange color.

INGREDIENTS

1g (2 lb) each pumpkin, sweet potatoes, and carrots

1 Tbsp sugar

1 Tbsp kosher salt

1/3 cup olive oil

1 onion

1 stalk celery

nutmeg, freshly ground

1/2 cup chives, finely chopped

2 cups milk

1 cup whipping cream

salt to taste

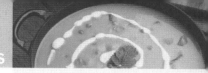

POTTAGE (VEGETABLE) SOUP

Eitan Ben-Elisha

Place all vegetables in a large pot. Add water, soup powder, oil, lemon juice, salt and pepper. Bring to a boil, then simmer until vegetables are tender. When the soup is almost done, thicken the soup with a mixture of flour and water. Add coriander.

INGREDIENTS

2 potatoes, diced
2 carrots, diced
1 onion, diced
2 zucchinis, diced
1/4 cabbage, sliced
1 tomato, chopped
8 to 10 cups water
2 Tbsp oil
juice of 1 lemon
salt, pepper, chicken
soup powder, to taste
flour to thicken soup
1 Tbsp coriander

RICH PUMPKIN SOUP

Yossi Citron

Put all the vegetables in a pot and cover with water. Add soup powder, salt, pepper, paprika, and for those with a sweet tooth, sugar. Cook until the vegetables are soft, then blend with a stick blender. Garnish with sunflower seeds.

INGREDIENTS

1g (2 lbs) pumpkin, cut in chunks
1 potato, cut in chunks
2 carrots, cut in chunks
2 Tbsp soup powder
salt and pepper
1 Tbsp sweet paprika
1 tsp sugar, optional
sunflower seeds

INGREDIENTS

500g (1 lb) split peas

1 leek, sliced

1 celeriac
(celery root), halved

8 cups water

salt and pepper

12 sausages, coarsely
sliced or vegetarian
sausages such as
Tivol

SNERT (SPLIT PEA SOUP)

Avinoam Hershler   the Netherlands

Bring peas, vegetables, and water to boil. Season with salt and pepper. Cook for 1 hour. Remove froth as it forms. Leave the pot uncovered to help prevent boiling over. When the peas have turned to paste, add the sausages. Simmer 10-20 minutes. This recipe can be made without sausages, if desired.

INGREDIENTS

1 onion, diced

1 sweet potato, diced

2 zucchinis, diced

1 cup split peas

1 Tbsp soup powder

salt and pepper to
taste

SPLIT PEA SOUP

Ohad Polak

Sauté onion until golden brown. Add vegetables and water. Bring to boil. Add peas, reboil, and simmer 1 hour until peas are soft. Blend and season. Add 2 more cups of water and season to taste.

SWEDISH FRUIT SOUP

Elaine Beychok

Combine grape juice, water, dried fruit, raisins, apples, lemon slice, and cinnamon in large pot. Bring to a boil, reduce heat, and add jello. Simmer for 30 minutes, stirring often. Add more water if needed. Serve hot or cold. Makes 6 servings.

INGREDIENTS

4 cups grape juice

4 cups water

500g (1 lb) mixed dried fruit (prunes, apricots, pineapple)

1/2 cup raisins

4 medium apples, peeled and sliced

1 lemon slice

1 stick cinnamon

1 box cherry instant jello

MATZAH BALLS

Naomi Freudenberger

Mix ingredients in order. Refrigerate at least 30 minutes. Boil 5 cups of water with a teaspoon of salt. Form balls from batter and place in boiling water. Cook for 30 minutes on medium flame. Serve with chicken soup.

INGREDIENTS

4 eggs beaten well, preferably with a mixer

1/2 cup water

1/3 cup oil

1 tsp salt

1 cup matzah meal

SESAME BROCCOLI SALAD

Alissa Fried Harbater

Steam broccoli florets until crispy/tender, about 5 minutes. Cool. Stir sesame seeds over medium heat until golden, about 5 minutes. Cool. Whisk soy sauce, vinegar, oil, and honey until well blended. Season to taste with salt and pepper. If using, add dash of chili sauce. Mix broccoli, red pepper, water chestnuts, and half of the sesame seeds into dressing. Let marinate at least 30 minutes at room temperature, tossing occasionally. To serve, pour into bowl and sprinkle with remaining sesame seeds. Serves 6.

INGREDIENTS

4 cups broccoli florets (2 large bunches)

2 Tbsp soy sauce

2 Tbsp rice vinegar

2 Tbsp sesame oil

2 Tbsp honey

1/2 cup sesame seeds

salt and pepper to taste

water chestnuts, sliced (optional)

1 red pepper, diced (optional)

dash of chinese chili sauce (optional)

CABBAGE AND ALMOND SALAD

Kibbutz Netiv HaLamed Hey Catering

Rena | 02 377 3790

SALAD
Cut the cabbage in small pieces. Put the almonds in the oven and bake until crisp.

DRESSING
Mix dressing ingredients together. Pour over cabbage. Top with almonds.

SALAD

1 small cabbage, chopped

1 cup almonds, chopped

DRESSING

2 Tbsp soy sauce

2 Tbsp vinegar

1 Tbsp sugar

1 Tbsp oil

CELERIAC SALAD

Elisheva Hershler

INGREDIENTS

1 large celery root, grated

3 red apples or sour apples, grated

juice of 1/2 lemon

1/2 tsp sugar

This is an oil-free Yekkish recipe. It is a good recipe for the end of the winter/early spring when large and young celery roots are in season.

Mix all salad ingredients quickly to ensure apples do not oxidize. Even if the apples do go brown, the salad still tastes great!

CORN SALAD

Tania Cohen

SALAD

2 cans corn

1 cucumber, chopped

2 pickles, chopped

1 red pepper, chopped

1 small onion, chopped

DRESSING

3 Tbsp oil

2 Tbsp lemon juice

1/2 tsp salt

1/4 tsp pepper

dash thyme

1/2 tsp mustard

SALAD

Cut vegetables into bite-sized pieces.

DRESSING

Mix and pour over salad.

COUSCOUS SALAD

Rachel Epstein

SALAD

Prepare couscous according to instructions on package. Add remaining ingredients.

DRESSING

Combine ingredients. Mix well and add to couscous salad.

SALAD

1 pkg couscous

3 scallions, chopped

1 red pepper, chopped

1 yellow pepper, chopped

1 cup canned chickpeas, drained

handful of raisins

DRESSING

1/2 cup olive oil

1/2 cup lemon juice

2 cloves garlic, minced

2 tsp coriander, optional

1 tsp Dijon mustard

1 tsp salt

black pepper, to taste

DELI SALAD

Daniella Slasky

Combine salad ingredients in a bowl. Shake dressing ingredients together and pour over salad.

SALAD

2 kinds of lettuce

200g (8 oz) sun-dried tomatoes

200g (8 oz) pine nuts

10 slices of packaged turkey, cut into strips

10 slices of pastrami, cut into strips

croutons

DRESSING

1/4 cup honey

1/2 cup sugar

1/4 cup red wine vinegar

1 Tbsp Dijon mustard

3/4 cup oil

FENNEL SALAD

Hannah Ido

A colorful dish and a feast for the eyes!

Julienne (cut into fine sticks) all the vegetables into 3 cm (1 inch) lengths. Add oil, vinegar, sugar, and salt.

INGREDIENTS

3 carrots
2-3 celery stalks
2 fennel bulbs
1 red pepper
1 Tbsp oil
2 Tbsp vinegar
1 tsp sugar
salt to taste

MORE THAN JUST LETTUCE SALAD

Yael Ben Pazi

Place all of the salad ingredients in a bowl.

Mix dressing ingredients and heat in microwave for one minute or until the sugar has melted. Cool. Pour on vegetables just before serving.

SALAD

1 lettuce, washed, torn to pieces
2 cucumbers, unpeeled and diced
1 large handful frozen peas
strips of dry figs
mixed nuts (pecans, walnuts, cashews, sugared pecans)
1 handful dried cranberries
fresh mushrooms, optional
chives or basil, optional

DRESSING

4 Tbsp olive oil
2 Tbsp white wine vinegar
2 Tbsp sugar
pinch of salt
2 Tbsp soy sauce

MANDARIN SALAD

Shellie Davis

Place lettuce in bowl and then remaining ingredients on top. Pour dressing over salad immediately before serving.

SALAD

1 head romaine lettuce

1 can mandarin oranges, drained

1 medium onion, chopped

1/2 cup slivered almonds (or more if desired)

handful of dried cranberries

DRESSING

2 Tbsp red wine vinegar

1/2 cup oil

2 Tbsp sugar

1 Tbsp lemon juice

1 tsp onion powder

MARKET SALAD

Liraz Infeld

A merchant at the Mahane Yehuda market in Jerusalem gave this recipe to me.

Place all ingredients in bowl and mix. Rocket leaves may be replaced with mixed young greens.

INGREDIENTS

lettuce, cut or torn

bunch of rocket leaves (arugula)

pomegranate seeds

olive oil

lemon juice

salt and pepper

SALAD

3 cups cooked brown rice

1/2 bunch
parsley, chopped

4 sticks celery, thinly sliced

5-6 scallions, green and white parts, thinly sliced

100g (3 1/2 oz) cashew nuts

DRESSING

1/2 cup olive oil

2 Tbsp lemon juice

4 Tbsp soy sauce

RICE SALAD

Esther Margolis

Place the rice in a large bowl. Add the celery, scallions, parsley, and cashew nuts. Mix all the ingredients for the dressing and pour on the salad. Serve at room temperature.

INGREDIENTS

500g (1 lb) noodles, cooked and drained

1 lb salami,
cut into chunks

1 red pepper, diced

1 green pepper, diced

2-3 onions, diced

1 package fresh mushrooms, sliced

1-2 fresh
tomatoes, diced

Ken's brand (or similar) Lite Italian Salad Dressing

SALAMI PASTA SALAD

Toby Curwin

This recipe has been a favorite in our family for years; it's extremely tasty, easy, and versatile. You can add or subtract amounts and types of vegetables to suit your family's individual taste. Here's how we do it.

Sauté the salami chunks until slightly darkened on both sides. Remove salami from pan, and sauté onions, peppers, and mushrooms in leftover salami fat. When vegetables are tender, remove from heat. Toss together noodles, cooked vegetables, salami, fresh tomatoes, and salad dressing. Serve hot or cold.

FRESH SPINACH AND FRUIT SALAD

Alissa Fried Harbater

Rinse the spinach well and rip. Combine all dressing ingredients and shake well. Toss with salad 15 minutes before serving.

1 bag fresh spinach

1 basket fresh strawberries, sliced

100g (3 oz) dried apple slices, cut in half

3 Tbsp olive oil

5 Tbsp honey

3 cloves garlic, crushed

3 Tbsp wine vinegar

1/2 tsp salt

1/4 tsp pepper

1 Tbsp sugar

SPINACH AND STRAWBERRY SALAD

Joy Gris

Mix the dressing and chill.
Toss dressing with salad immediately before serving.
Makes enough for 2 salads.

1 head fresh spinach or

1 romaine lettuce

2 kiwi, peeled and sliced

4 cups strawberries, hulled and sliced

2 Tbsp sesame seeds

1 Tbsp poppy seeds

1/4 cup cider vinegar

1/2 cup oil

1/4 cup sugar

1 Worcestershire sauce

1/2 tsp paprika

4 tsp minced onion

INGREDIENTS

1 basket bean sprouts

1 red pepper sliced into strips

1 yellow pepper, sliced into strips

1 orange pepper, sliced into strips

2 carrots, grated

vinegar

olive oil

soy sauce

salt

pepper

INTERESTING SPROUT SALAD

Rachel Tzur

Place all the vegetables in a bowl. Pour 3 tablespoons each of vinegar, olive oil, and soy sauce, and season with salt and pepper. Mix well and serve.

INGREDIENTS

200 g (7 oz) bulghur wheat

1 - 1 1/2 cup water

1/2 cup olive oil

2 bunches parsley

1 cucumber

1 tomato

1/2 red or white onion

1 clove garlic, crushed

juice from 1/2 a lemon

LEBANESE TABOULEH SALAD

Anonymous

This salad has many variations, the difference between them being quantities and spicing. This recipe was arrived at after many taste testings at home.

Mix the bulghur with the olive oil and water. Cook in a microwave at maximum power for 4 minutes. Remove and fluff with a fork. Taste. If the granules are still hard, add a 1/2 cup of water and cook in the microwave for 2 minutes. Fluff with a fork. Rinse the parsley and remove hard stalks. Finely chop the parsley using a sharp knife, not a food processor, and add to the bulghur. Finely dice the cucumber, tomato, and onion, then add to the bulghur. Spice with lemon juice, garlic, and salt. Mix well. Refrigerate immediately or it may not make it to the table!

TABOULEH SALAD

Avigail Rachamim

Soak the bulghur in water and cover for two hours or until the bulghur has soaked up the water. Finely chop the parsely, mint, and scallions. Combine all the ingredients and mix well.

INGREDIENTS

2 cups bulghur
1/2 bunch parsley
1/2 bunch mint
1/2 bunch scallions
3 Tbsp olive oil
vinegar, to taste
salt, to taste

TOMATO AND BLACK OLIVE SALAD

Esther Margolis

In a bowl, place the tomatoes, peppers, almonds, and black olives. Dress with a small amount of olive oil, lemon juice, salt, and pepper.

INGREDIENTS

4 tomatoes, diced
4 red peppers, diced
1/2 cup sliced black olives, sliced
1/2 cup almonds, cut into thirds
lemon juice
olive oil
salt and pepper

TROPICAL SALAD

Nurit Aharoni | France

Mix the ingredients well and pour over the salad.

SALAD

150g (5 oz) mixed "baby" salad greens
8 leaves romaine lettuce
1 mango, cubed
1 avocado, cubed
1 red pepper, cubed

DRESSING

1 Tbsp balsamic vinegar
1 Tbsp olive oil
a pinch of ground green pepper
1 tsp salt

SALAD

1 head of
iceberg lettuce

2 cucumbers, sliced

1 green and/or
red pepper

1 carrot, grated

mushrooms, sliced

cherry tomatoes,
halved

salty cheese, cubed

fruit (peaches,
lychees or whatever
you like)

DRESSING

1/3-1/2 cup olive oil

1 Tbsp onion soup
powder

2 Tbsp sugar

sliced almonds

2 tsp toasted sesame
seeds

OFFICERS' VEGETABLE SALAD

Liat Citron

This is a great salad. I got this recipe at an officers' army base and it has an unusual combination of ingredients. The ingredients can be varied since the important part is the dressing.

SALAD
Combine the ingredients in a bowl.

DRESSING
Toast the sesame seeds in oil. Remove from flame as soon as the seeds turn golden. Be careful not to burn them. Mix the olive oil, onion soup powder and sugar. Pour over the vegetables 30 minutes before serving. Sprinkle the almonds and sesame seeds over the salad or serve separately. Eat up and no arguing.

BATTER-DIPPED FISH

Sue Epstein | Author of "Budget Cooking-Elegant Dining" and "Simply Delicious"

The secret to crisp (not soggy) fried fish is to have the oil hot enough. When you can drop a small piece of bread into the oil and it browns almost immediately, the oil is hot enough. Another way to test the oil is to put the handle of a wooden spoon or wooden chopstick into the oil. If it bubbles around the handle, it's hot enough.

Heat the oil in a deep pan to about 200C (400F). Cut the fish into approximately 7 x 2-inch wedges. With a mixer, blend the flour, water, egg, sugar, and salt. Dip each fillet into the batter, coating generously, and quickly drop into the oil. Fry each fillet until dark golden brown, about 5 minutes. Remove from the oil and place on paper towels or metal rack to drain.

SWEET AND SOUR CARP

Tzippy Grunstein

STOCK

2 carrots, sliced

2 onions, sliced

salt, pepper, paprika, sugar

3-4 lemon slices

water

FISH

carp, steaks

1-2 tsp vinegar

Combine stock ingredients and bring to boil. Season to taste. Simmer for 1 hour. Add carp and vinegar to stock. Cook for an additional 45 minutes.

DENISE WITH OLIVE OIL, LEMON, AND ROSEMARY

La Guta Restaurant | Jerusalem

Preheat oven to 180C (350F).

Heat 1 Tbsp olive oil in non-stick skillet. When oil is hot, coat fish with flour and fry 3 minutes per side. Remove from skillet and place in oven for 7 minutes. Mix lemon juice with remaining 1 Tbsp oil, rosemary, and seasonings. Place fish on serving dish and top with sauce.

INGREDIENTS

2 fillets of Bream ("Denise")

1 sprig rosemary, chopped

2 Tbsp olive oil, divided

1 Tbsp lemon juice

salt

pepper

FISH FILLET IN OLIVE OIL AND HERBS

Courtesy of Chef Yuval Cochavi |

Olive Restaurant | 36 Emek Refaim St. |

Jerusalem

Heat oil in frying pan. Place fish fillet in pan, skin side up. Fry 2 minutes on each side. Add all other ingredients to the pan, bring to a boil, and cook a further 3 minutes. Place fish on serving dish and pour sauce on top.

INGREDIENTS

2 fish fillets (Mullet, St. Peter's Fish, Bream)

3 Tbsp olive oil

1 Tbsp parsley, chopped

1 sprig thyme, chopped

2 cloves garlic, minced

1 cup dry white wine

juice of 1 lemon

1 tsp capers

1/2 tsp salt

1/2 tsp coarsely ground pepper

JAZZED-UP GEFILTE FISH

Daphne Kupietzky

OPTION ONE

1 loaf of gefilte fish

French pastry dough

1 egg

sesame seeds

OPTION TWO

1 loaf gefilte fish

brown sugar

onion powder

garlic powder

1/4 bag of frozen spinach

French pastry dough

OPTION THREE

1 loaf gefilte fish

1/4 cup prepared curry sauce

1 cup marinara sauce

OPTION ONE

Thaw a loaf of gefilte fish and mash it. Roll out dough and fill with gefilte fish. Shape into a loaf, brush with egg and sprinkle with sesame seeds. Bake until golden. Serve with horseradish, mushroom sauce, or any other sauce you like!

OPTION TWO

Thaw fish and add spices. Defrost the spinach and drain, and add to fish mixture. Then follow the same instructions as the above recipe.

OPTION THREE

Unwrap loaf of fish and place in baking dish. Pour sauces on top of fish. Bake until the fish looks golden. Serve warm on Friday night.

MOROCCAN FISH

Joy Epstein

INGREDIENTS

fish fillets (Nile perch, salmon, or any thick fish)

3 Tbsp tomato paste

8 cloves garlic, mashed

1/4 cup olive oil

1 Tbsp cumin

1 tsp turmeric

1 tsp salt

1/2 tsp pepper

juice of 1 lemon

2 Tbsp water

1/2 cup chopped fresh cilantro, divided

1 cup chickpeas

2 chili peppers, slit in half and seeded

Preheat oven to 180C (350F).

Lay fish fillets in 9x13 pan. Mix all of the above except last 2 ingredients into a paste. Spread paste over fish. Pour chickpeas over fish. Rest chili peppers on top of the chickpeas. Sprinkle another 1/4 cup chopped cilantro on top. Cover and bake for 1 hour.

BAKED BREADED NILE PERCH

Ettie Davies

Preheat oven to 200C (400F). Crunch the soup mix with a rolling pin. Combine the soup mix, breadcrumbs, and pepper on a plate. Mix egg and water in a shallow dish. Dip fish into the egg mixture. Coat with the crumb mixture. Place fish on a greased baking sheet. Drizzle with margarine. Bake for 20 minutes or until the fish is browned and flaky.

INGREDIENTS

1kg (2 lbs)
Nile perch fish

3 Tbsp onion
soup mix

2/3 cup dry bread-crumbs, cornflake crumbs or matzo meal

1/8 tsp pepper

1 egg

2 Tbsp water

2 Tbsp margarine, melted

SALMON WITH CREAM SAUCE

Pninat Hayam Restaurant | Jerusalem | 02 671 8376

SALMON

Sprinkle salt and white pepper over the fish. Dredge each slice in flour. Melt butter with the oil in a frying pan. Fry each piece on both sides. Set aside.

SAUCE

Combine the milk with the soup powder in a saucepan. Add the garlic, salt, and pepper. Bring to a boil. Stir in the yellow cheese. Add the mushrooms and wine. Cook over low flame until creamy, stirring constantly with a wooden spoon to prevent clumps. Pour the sauce over the fish. Grate the walnuts over the sauce-covered fish and serve.

SALMON

4 salmon steaks or fillets

1/2 tsp kosher salt

1/4 tsp white pepper

flour for breading

50g (1/4 cup) butter

1/2 cup oil

SAUCE

2 1/4 cup milk

1 Tbsp parve chicken soup powder

1 garlic clove, mashed

salt and pepper to taste

50g (1/4 cup) yellow cheese, grated

fresh mushrooms, sliced

1/2 cup white wine

walnuts

SMOKEY SALMON

Aliza Beinhaker

INGREDIENTS

4 pieces of salmon fillet

1/4 cup orange juice

2 Tbsp lemon juice

1 1/2 Tbsp brown sugar

3/4 tsp chili powder

1/4 tsp cinnamon

1/2 tsp salt

tsp cumin

Marinate salmon in orange and lemon juices.
Rub dry ingredients on salmon and broil.

TUNA SALAD SUSHI TORTILLAS

Sue Epstein | Author of "Budget Cooking-Elegant Dining" and "Simply Delicious"

INGREDIENTS

1 12-oz can chunk light tuna in water

1/4 cup mayonnaise

1/2 cup celery, chopped

2 10-inch flour tortillas

6 carrot strips

In a mixing bowl, stir together tuna, mayonnaise, and celery, breaking up any large chunks of tuna. Place half of the tuna salad on each tortilla in a line slightly below the center of the tortilla. Make a line of carrots strips along the middle of the tuna salad. Roll into a cylinder, sushi fashion. Trim ends and slice each roll into 6 pieces.

PICKLED CORNED BEEF WITH SAUCE

Mataam Chafetz Chaim | Jerusalem |
02 623 2839

BEEF

Boil a pot of water. Add the corned beef. Cook for
1 hour and 15 minutes on a medium flame. Remove
from water. Cool. When cold, slice. Refrigerate. Reserve
some of the cooking water so the meat won't dry out
when reheated.

SAUCE

Boil all ingredients until the sugar is dissolved. If serving
this for Shabbat lunch, it can be served at room
temperature, otherwise, serve it hot together with
the beef.

BEEF

1 Pickled Corned Beef
Roast

SAUCE

1 cup brown sugar

2 tsp mustard

5 Tbsp ketchup

2 tsp oil

2 tsp vinegar

LAMB STEW

Maya Edri

Fry the meat in oil until brown. Add onion. Add spices
and water and cook five minutes. Add lentils, cook
1 hour. Add raisins, simmer 20 minutes. Season with salt
and pepper. When the stew is done, you may add lemon
juice and honey.

INGREDIENTS

1kg (2 lbs) lamb or
beef, diced

1 onion, chopped

1/2 tsp ginger

1/2 tsp cinnamon

1 tsp cumin

5 cups water

1 cup lentils

2 cups raisins,
soaked overnight in
1 cup wine

salt

pepper

soup powder to taste

lemon juice

honey (optional)

LAMB TAJIN WITH JERUSALEM ARTICHOKE

Courtesy of Darna Restaurant | Jerusalem

The beauty of this dish is in its simple preparation.

Slice meat off the bone into 4 cm pieces, and place in the center of the Tajin (special Middle Eastern crock pot). Add chopped onion, garlic and parsley, spices, oil and water. Cook over medium heat for 2 hours. Peel the Jerusalem artichokes and parboil in salted water. Add to Tajin about 30 minutes before the end of cooking time. The dish is served in the center of the table in its special cooking dish.

INGREDIENTS

800g (1 1/2 lbs) lamb shoulder

2 onions, chopped

2 garlic gloves, crushed

small bunch parsley, chopped

1/2 tsp salt

1/2 tsp white pepper

1/2 tsp ground ginger

few strands saffron

1/2 cup olive oil

1 tomato, peeled and diced

1 cup water

500g (1 lb) Jerusalem artichoke

MEATBALLS WITH POMEGRANATES AND ALMONDS

Sima Navon

A Tu b'Shvat Recipe because it uses one of the Seven Species. Inspired by a Persian recipe in C. Marks's "Sephardic Cooking"

Mix meat, grated onion, salt, and pepper, and shape into small meatballs. Heat oil in a skillet and brown the meatballs so that they retain their shape. Remove the meatballs and then, with the remaining oil, fry the chopped onions until light brown. Add the almonds and the meatballs.

Add the sauce ingredients to the pan and slowly bring to a boil. If necessary, mix occasionally so that the bottom doesn't burn. Lower the flame and cook covered for 1 hour, stirring gently now and then. Serve hot on a bed of rice.

MEATBALLS

1kg (2 lb) chopped meat

1 medium onion, grated

1 tsp salt

dash of pepper

1 Tbsp oil

2 medium onions, chopped

2 cups almonds, shelled, toasted, and ground

SAUCE

1/4 tsp turmeric

1/3 cup pomegranate juice concentrate

2 cups water

1/2 cup tomato paste

1 cup dried apricots, soaked in water for 2 hours

1 tsp baharat (allspice)

MEATBALLS WITH SWEET AND SOUR SAUCE

Alissa Fried Harbater

Mix meat, egg, onion, and breadcrumbs. Form into balls. In pot, heat ketchup, lemon juice, and jelly to simmer. Add in meatballs. Cook on low heat for 1-1 1/2 hours.

INGREDIENTS

1kg (2 lbs) chopped meat

1 onion, grated

1 egg

handful of breadcrumbs

1 1/2 cup ketchup

1 1/4 cup plum jelly

2 Tbsp lemon juice

MEAT LASAGNE

Nurit Cohen

An Italian recipe passed down from my mother.

TOMATO SAUCE
Fry the onion in oil. Add the meat and fry until brown. Add the crushed tomatoes, tomato paste, water, herbs, and spices. Bring to a boil and simmer for five minutes. The sauce should not get too thick.

BECHAMEL SAUCE
Bring 1 cup water and margarine to a boil. Mix the flour with the second cup of the water and add to the pot. Add the nutmeg, salt, and pepper. Bring to a boil while stirring constantly.

LASAGNE
Preheat oven to 180C (350F).

Oil a baking pan and line with a layer of lasagne noodles. Pour a layer of tomato sauce on the lasagne noodles and then a layer of bechamel sauce on top and then place another layer of lasagne noodles on top. Repeat the process finishing with tomato sauce and bechamel sauce. Bake for 15 minutes or until the noodles are soft but not dry.

LASAGNE

500g (1 lb) lasagne noodles, uncooked

TOMATO SAUCE

250g (1 lb) chopped meat

1 onion, chopped

1/2 cup oil

800g (1 1/2 lb) crushed tomatoes

100g (3 1/2 oz) tomato paste

1 cup water

parsley, chopped

basil, to taste

oregano

salt and pepper

BECHAMEL SAUCE

1/4 cup margarine

2 cups water, divided

3 Tbsp flour

1 tsp nutmeg

salt and pepper

31

MEAT & MUSHROOM ROLL

Sura Avni

Preheat oven to 180C (350F).

Sauté mushrooms and onions in oil. In a bowl, mix chopped meat, breadcrumbs, and egg. Place meat mixture into frying pan with the mushrooms and onions. Sauté until brown. Thaw pastry sheet, unroll it, and cut in half. Place meat mixture in the center and roll. Put in greased tin. Bake for 45 minutes.

INGREDIENTS

3/4kg (1 1/2 lbs) chopped meat

3/4kg (1 1/2 lbs) fresh mushrooms

1 medium onion, chopped

1 Tbsp oil

1/2 cup bread crumbs

1 large egg

1 sheet puff pastry

LAHMASHIN | MEAT PASTIES

Miriam Weingrover | School Principal

Preheat oven to 180C (350F).

DOUGH
Mix all ingredients and form 18 balls of dough. Place on greased cookie sheet and set aside.

FILLING
Fry onion in oil until golden. Add beef and brown. Add remaining ingredients and simmer.

Flatten balls of dough with your hands onto the cookie sheet. Place one tablespoon of filling on each circle. You can leave the patties open or pinch closed in triangles. Bake for approximately 20 minutes.

Serves 6

DOUGH

4 cups flour

1 1/2 Tbsp yeast

salt

water, room temperature

FILLING

1 onion, grated

oil for frying

500g (1 lb) ground beef

1 can (26 oz) crushed tomatoes

sugar, to taste

lemon juice, to taste

MEAT PATTIES IN CARROT SAUCE

Eitam Yablowitz

PATTIES

Fry onion in oil until soft and add wine. Mix onion mixture with meat. Beat eggs with water and add to mixture. Add remaining ingredients. Mix well and let stand for 15 minutes to absorb flavors.

SAUCE

Heat oil in pot and fry onion until golden. Add carrots and steam on low heat. Pour in water and stir. Dilute soup powder and flour with boiling water. Add to pan along with soy sauce and pepper. Bring to boil and then simmer on low heat. Form small meatballs and slide gently into sauce. Cover pot and simmer for 30-35 minutes.

Makes 8 servings.

PATTIES

1kg (2 lbs) ground meat, turkey, or beef

1 Tbsp oil

1 medium onion, finely chopped

1 Tbsp dry white wine

3 eggs

2 Tbsp water

2 Tbsp self-rising flour

2 Tbsp bread crumbs

2 cloves of garlic, pressed

dash of salt

dash of pepper

SAUCE

2 Tbsp oil

1 onion, finely chopped

2 carrots, finely chopped

2 cups water

1 Tbsp chicken soup powder

1 tsp flour

1/2 cup boiling water

1 Tbsp soy sauce

dash of white pepper

6 potatoes

4 zucchini

4 tomatoes

2 eggplants

STUFFING

1kg (2 lbs) chopped meat

2 eggs

1 handful of bread-crumbs

1 tsp salt

1/2 tsp pepper

1 tsp paprika

SAUCE

400g (14 oz) tomato paste

8 cups water

1 tsp salt

1/2 tsp pepper

2 tsp cumin

MEDIAS

Nitsan, Re'ut, Tomar and Ariel Malchi | Spain

In Spanish "medias" means halves. Grandma Miriam, my mother's grandmother, made Aliyah from Morocco more than 90 years ago. In the Old City of Jerusalem she met my great grandfather, Yitzchak, who made Aliya from Turkey. Grandma learned to cook many delicious foods from her friends in the Spaniolt (Sephardim who speak Ladino) in order to make Grandpa happy with food that he had grown up with.

VEGETABLES

Cut the potatoes in half. "Dig a hole" in each half, cut the zucchini in half a "dig a canal" in each half. Remove the inside of the tomatoes and cut the eggplant into "sandwiches", that is, thick slices slit through the middle but not to the end.

STUFFING

Mix all the ingredients together and fill the vegetables with the meat mixture. Dip in egg and fry.

SAUCE

Mix all the ingredients in a large pot. Gently place the fried stuffed vegetables (medias) in the pot. First put in the potatoes and then the other vegetables on top. Cook together for 45-60 minutes

STUFFED ROAST BEEF

Hess Meat Delicacies Restaurant, Bistro,
Shop | Heleni HaMalka 9 | Jerusalem

Mix all the stuffing ingredients together. Cut roast in the
middle with a long knife down the length of the roast to
make a pocket for the stuffing. Stuff, and then sew the
hole. Season the beef roast with sweet paprika and
French mustard.

Put in preheated 220C (425F) oven for approximately
30 minutes. After it gets a nice brown color, reduce heat
to 150C (300F). Add the red wine and a cup of water.
Cover with aluminum foil and bake for approximately
2 more hours until the inside of the beef reaches a
temperature of 70C (160F), using a meat thermometer
to check. Slice into approximately 8 slices and serve with
mashed potatoes or rice.

To serve Friday night, let the inside temperature of
the roast only reach 60C (140F), then lower the oven
to 85C (185F) to keep the roast warm. Keep it covered
so it won't dry out until your guests return from Shul,
bringing the inside temperature slowly to the needed
70C (160F).

STUFFED BEEF

1 1/2kg (3 lbs) beef
roast (Tzli Katef #5),
from the premium cut
side with a small
nerve in the middle

sweet paprika

French mustard

1 cup sweet red
Kiddush wine

STUFFING

150g (5 oz)
pitted dried prunes

150g (5 oz) chopped
or minced chicken
liver

100g (3 oz) fried
onions

100g (3 oz) bread
crumbs

2 raw eggs

a little soup or water,
to bind

a drop of Israeli
brandy

1/2 tsp cinnamon

PEPPER STEAK

SWEET AND SOUR FRENCH ROAST

Sara Weinstein

Preheat oven to 180C (350F).

Combine all of the ingredients except the roast in a small pot, and simmer until sugar dissolves. Cool a bit, then pour over roast. Marinate for at least 8 hours if possible. Bake covered until roast is done, 1-2 hours depending on your oven. Cover it very well, and check frequently to make sure sauce does not dry up and start to burn. You may have to add water.

INGREDIENTS

large roast 2kg (4 lb), number 5 or 6

2 onions, cut up

3 cloves garlic, crushed or sliced

1/2 cup brown sugar

1 cup ketchup

3/4 cup balsamic vinegar

2 tsp soy sauce

2 tsp apricot jelly

PEPPER STEAK

Mataam Chafetz Chaim | Jerusalem | 02 623 2839

Brown the strips of pepper steak in a little bit of oil. Add any or all of the vegetables to the meat. Combine the sauce ingredients and pour over the steak and vegetables. Cook 30-40 minutes on low flame. Serve over rice. This dish freezes well.

PEPPER STEAK

1kg (2 lbs) Pepper Steak, cut in strips

VEGETABLES

red, yellow, or green peppers, sliced

1 can or fresh mushrooms

a few cherry tomatoes, optional

baby corn, optional

SAUCE

1 cup boiling water

4 Tbsp onion soup powder

1 Tbsp brown sugar

1 Tbsp soy or tamari sauce

STEAK WITH GARLIC SAUCE

Courtesy of La Guta Restaurant
Chef Guta Ben-Simchon

Preheat oven to 180C (350F).

Heat grill pan or non-stick skillet. Pour in olive oil. When oil is hot, gently place steak in skillet and reduce heat. Grill to desired doneness, then transfer to 250C (450F) oven for 8 minutes. Heat small pan and add olive oil. Brown garlic cloves, then add red wine. Add sugar to taste. Cook for a few minutes until reduced by half. Place steak on serving dish and pour over sauce and garlic.

INGREDIENTS

250g (9 oz) steak
garlic cloves, peeled
1 cup good red wine
olive oil
sugar

APRICOT CHICKEN

Sarit Herbst

Preheat oven to 180C (350F).

Mix all sauce ingredients in jar. Dip chicken pieces in sauce. Bake for 75 minutes.

INGREDIENTS

1 chicken, cut into eighths

1/2 cup apricot preserves

3-4 Tbsp soy sauce

3-4 Tbsp honey

2-3 cloves garlic, crushed

CHICKEN CHOW MEIN

Tzippy Grunstein

2 cups cooked chicken

3 stalks celery

2 medium onions

1 small can sliced mushrooms or 3-4 sliced fresh mushrooms

1 tsp salt

1/4 cup oil

1 cup water

1 Tbsp flour

1 tsp black pepper

chinese noodles

Drain mushrooms, and reserve liquid. Sauté celery and onions oil for 5-10 minutes. Add mushrooms to celery and onions. Add chicken and water and heat. Mix flour with liquid from mushrooms. Add to the skillet and cook uncovered for 5 minutes until thick. Season with salt and pepper. Serve over rice and top with Chinese noodles. One can substitute tuna for chicken and leave out salt.

CHICKEN WITH CUMIN

Shoshana Rothkoff

1 medium chicken, cut up

1 large onion, sliced

1 large stalk celery, sliced

2 carrots, sliced

1/4 tsp black pepper

1 tsp cumin

1 tsp paprika

1 cup white wine

1 cup orange juice

3 Tbsp oil

1/2 cup raisins

Preheat oven to 180C (350F).

Place chicken pieces in deep baking pan. Place the vegetables on chicken. Add pepper, cumin, and paprika. Mix together wine, oil, and orange juice, and pour on chicken. Cover and bake for an hour. Add raisins and continue baking for half an hour, uncovered.

CHICKEN WITH FIGS

Adina Sussman

A Tu b'Shvat recipe, because it uses one of the Seven Species

Brown the chicken in the oil using a large pot or skillet. Add the water and the remaining ingredients. Bring to a boil and then simmer covered for 20 minutes. Remove cover and cook on a high flame until the water boils out and you are left with a thick sauce. Serve hot on a bed of rice.

INGREDIENTS

1 chicken, cut into 6-8 pieces

2 Tbsp vegetable oil

1 cup water

15 dried figs (approximately), sliced into thin strips

1 lemon, sliced into thin strips

5 garlic cloves, sliced into thin strips

10 sprigs coriander, chopped

1/2 tsp turmeric

salt and pepper to taste

CHICKEN IN HONEY MUSTARD SAUCE

Sarit Herbst

Preheat oven to 180C (350F).

Prepare sauce of mustard, honey, and water. Dip chicken in sauce and bake for approximately 75 minutes, until brown. Baste the chicken while baking.

INGREDIENTS

1 chicken, cut into eighths

3 to 4 Tbsp Dijon mustard with seeds

3 to 4 Tbsp honey

1/3 cup water

CHICKEN IN MUSTARD SAUCE

Matia Tur-Paz

Preheat oven to 180C (350F).

Prepare sauce with all the ingredients (mustard through egg). Dip chicken in sauce and place in dish. Sprinkle breadcrumbs over chicken and dab with margarine. Pour water into the pan. Bake 1 hour covered and 1/2 hour uncovered.

INGREDIENTS

1 chicken, cut into eighths

1 heaping Tbsp mustard

1 tsp cumin

4 or 5 cloves garlic, crushed

1/4 tsp black pepper

1/2 tsp paprika

1 egg

breadcrumbs (enough for lightly topping the chicken)

margarine (1 dab per piece of chicken)

3/4 cup water

CHICKEN IN TOBEE'S SPECIAL SAUCE

Tobee Weisel

Combine Italian dressing, white wine, and mustard in bowl. Drop and coat all schnitzel pieces in sauce mixture. Marinate at least 1 hour. Place coated schnitzel on broiler pan and broil 10 minutes. Remove from oven; turn and baste. Broil additional 10 minutes on other side. Serve immediately. Can also be served cold.

INGREDIENTS

8 pieces chicken schnitzel

1/4 cup creamy Italian dressing (Osem)

1/3 cup white wine

1/4 cup mustard

CHICKEN WITH PLUMS

Matia Tur-Paz

Preheat oven to 180C (350F).

Mix plum juice with soy sauce and onion soup mix. Dip chicken pieces in sauce and place in baking tray. Bake for 1 hour covered and an additional 1/2 hour uncovered.

INGREDIENTS

1 chicken, cut into eighths

1 can plums, drained and sliced

2 Tbsp soy sauce

2 Tbsp onion soup powder

SHYKE'S SECRET CHICKEN

Shyke El Ami

Preheat oven to 180C (350F).

Mix all ingredients except chicken. Pour over chicken. Bake uncovered, for 45 minutes. Remove from oven and baste chicken with sauce. Pour syrup or honey over chicken if desired. Grill for additional 15 minutes. All that's left is to lick your fingers!

INGREDIENTS

1 chicken, cut into eighths

1 Tbsp chicken soup powder

1 Tbsp mustard

3 Tbsp soy sauce

1 cup red wine

1 Tbsp olive oil

salt

pepper

optional: maple syrup or honey

HAWAIIAN CHICKEN

Naomi Berger

Naomi Berger

Preheat oven to 180C (350F).

Mix the last 5 ingredients and pour over chicken. Bake for approximately 1 hour until chicken browns, basting chicken periodically.

INGREDIENTS

INGREDIENTS

1 chicken, cut into eighths

1 cup crushed pineapple with juice

1/2 cup brown sugar

1 tsp ginger

dash garlic powder

1/4 cup soy sauce

PAN FRIED CHICKEN

Debbie Schiff

Preheat oven to 180C (350F).

Mix the spices into the flour. Dip pieces of chicken into the water and then into the seasoned flour. Place in baking pan coated with oil. Bake, uncovered, for 1 1/2 hours.

Tips: If the chicken is not browning, spray it with cooking spray. Chicken comes out better if made with the skin on.

INGREDIENTS

1 chicken, cut into eighths

2 Tbsp oil

bowl of water

2 cups flour

salt

pepper

garlic powder

onion powder

paprika

PASTRAMI-CHICKEN ROLL

Shellie Davis

Preheat oven to 180C (350F).

CHICKEN
Marinate chicken in Italian dressing.

COATING
Coat marinated cutlets in cornflake crumbs and roll with pastrami. Secure rolls with toothpicks if necessary, and arrange in a greased pan. Bake for 45 minutes covered, then 15 minutes uncovered.

INGREDIENTS

6 chicken cutlets

8 oz Italian dressing

6 slices pastrami

1 1/2 cups cornflake crumbs

ROASTED CHICKEN DINNER

Ellen Winetsky

Preheat oven to 200C (400F).

Place chicken in pan, along with the vegetables. Sprinkle chicken (both sides) and vegetables with rosemary, salt, pepper, garlic powder, and paprika. Pour wine into pan. Cook uncovered for 30 minutes. Lower heat to 180C (350F) and cook 1 hour more, lightly covered. Baste chicken every 20 minutes and add more wine as needed. There needs to be enough liquid to keep chicken juicy. If you prefer less wine, you can add chicken consommé instead.

INGREDIENTS

1 whole chicken

3 carrots, cut into chunks

2 onions, cut into quarters

3 potatoes, cut into chunks

rosemary, salt, pepper, garlic powder, paprika

1 1/2 cups white wine

TAJINE OF CHICKEN WITH PRUNES AND ALMONDS

Vita Friedman

INGREDIENTS

1.5kg (3 lbs) chicken pieces

2 Tbsp margarine or oil

1 medium onion, finely chopped

1 cup water

2 tsp cinnamon (more or less to taste)

1/2 tsp ginger or allspice

1/2 tsp pepper

salt

8 prunes, cut in half

1 Tbsp honey or sugar

1 cup whole almonds, toasted

In skillet, sauté onion in oil until tender but not brown. Add chicken and lightly brown. Mix water with cinnamon, ginger, pepper, and salt, and pour over chicken. Bring to boil. Cover the skillet and simmer 30 minutes. Add prunes, placing under the chicken, and bake for about 1 hour. When serving, add almonds.

TURKEY BREAST

Mataam Chafetz Chaim   Jerusalem

02 623 2839

TURKEY

1 whole turkey breast

onions, sliced

water

SAUCE

1/4 cup mustard

1/2 cup honey

3 Tbsp white wine

2 Tbsp soy sauce

garlic powder

Preheat oven to 180C (350F).

TURKEY

Place turkey breast on a bed of onions and add a little bit of water.

SAUCE

Mix the mustard and honey, and microwave until heated through. Add the wine, soy sauce, and garlic powder. Pour the sauce over the turkey breast. Cover and bake about 2 1/2 hours.

BLINTZ LOAF

2 250g containers
(16 oz) cottage
cheese

1/2 cup margarine,
melted

1 cup flour

1/2 cup sugar

1 tsp baking powder

6 eggs, beaten

TOPPING

Powdered sugar

BLINTZ LOAF

Plain & Fancy Catering, 654-0678

Preheat oven to 180C (350F).

BLINTZ LOAF

Melt margarine. Add rest of ingredients. Mix well. Bake in a greased 9x13 pan for 30-40 minutes.

TOPPING

Sprinkle powdered sugar over loaf just before serving. Serve hot.

INGREDIENTS

6 cups cubed bread,
crusts removed

12 eggs, beaten

1 cup buttermilk

1 cup milk

1/4 cup melted butter

1 Tbsp vanilla extract

cinnamon sugar, to
taste

BREAD CUSTARD SOUFFLE

Zahava Bogner

Preheat oven to 180C (350F).

Place cubed bread in greased 9x13 pan. Whisk together eggs, buttermilk, milk, melted butter, and vanilla extract. Allow bread to marinate in egg mixture for at least two hours. Before placing in oven, mix well and sprinkle with cinnamon sugar.

Bake for 45-50 minutes until souffle is puffed and golden brown. Serve with maple syrup, fresh fruit or jam.

CHEESE BLINTZES

COURTESY OF MA'AFE NE'EMAN CAFE

BLINTZES

Mix all ingredients into a smooth batter. Heat large frying pan and grease lightly. Pour enough mixture to cover pan and fry until golden. Turn out and continue frying blintzes, placing them in a pile.

FILLING

Mix together all ingredients. Place a spoonful of filling on each blintz, fold in edges and roll up. May be heated in oven or frying pan.

BLINTZES

500g (1 lb) flour

8 eggs

2 cup milk

2 cup water

1/4 cup oil

salt

sugar

FILLING

250g (8 oz) 5% white cheese

250g (8 oz) cream cheese

200g (7 oz) confectionary sugar

raisins

grated rind from 1 lemon

1 tsp good quality cognac

1 tsp vanilla extract

LAYERED EGGS AND POTATOES (DAIRY) – RUKUTKRUMPLE

Sarah Yosovich

Preheat oven to 180C (350F).

Boil the potatoes until they are soft and then peel them. Oil a baking pan with butter. Slice the potatoes and place them in the baking pan. Lightly salt. Pour 2 containers of sour cream on the potatoes and then arrange two sliced eggs. Repeat the process with the rest of the ingredients. Bake for an hour and a half.

INGREDIENTS

3kg (6 1/2 lbs) potatoes, unpeeled

4 containers sour cream 15% (3 1/2 cups)

5 hard-boiled eggs, sliced

butter

bread crumbs

salt

GNOCCHI

1kg (2 lbs) potatoes, boiled and skinned

300g (10 oz) flour

1 egg

30g (1 oz) butter

2 Tbsp grated Parmesan

a pinch of salt

black pepper

nutmeg

SAUCE

2 cups whipping cream

1/4 cup butter

bunch of chives, chopped

5 Tbsp grated Parmesan

salt

black pepper

nutmeg

GNOCCHI IN CREAM AND CHIVES SAUCE

Sofia, Inbal Hotel

GNOCCHI

Mash the potatoes to a smooth puree. Add egg, flour, butter, Parmesan, and seasoning. Gently knead to an even dough. Chill for an hour. Shape dough into finger thickness rolls and slice into 3/4 inch slices. Roll each slice with a fork to the shape of gnocchi. Bring a quart of water to the boil with a little salt, add the gnocchi, and cook until they float. Remove with a slotted spoon.

SAUCE

Bring the cream to the boil and reduce by half. Remove from heat, add butter, and stir to incorporate into cream. Add gnocchi and chives, stir, then sprinkle the Parmesan.

INGREDIENTS

1 onion, finely diced

oil for frying

250g (8.5 oz) tomato puree

1 cup water

dash of salt

dash of pepper

1 Tbsp oregano

500g (1 lb) cottage cheese

1 egg

200g (6.5 oz) yellow cheese

500g (1 lb) lasagna noodles

LASAGNA

Hazel Vahav

Preheat oven to 180C (350F).

TOMATO SAUCE

Fry onion in oil. Add tomato puree, water, salt, pepper and oregano. Bring to a boil, lower flame and simmer for 2-3 minutes.

CHEESE FILLING

In large bowl, mix cottage cheese, egg, and 2/3 of yellow cheese.

TO ASSEMBLE

Place a layer of noodles in pan, about 4 noodles across. Cover noodles with 1/3 of the tomato sauce and layer with 1/2 of the cheese filling. Repeat with noodle layer, tomato sauce, and cheese filling. Finish with third layer of noodles and top with sauce. Sprinkle remaining yellow cheese on top. Bake for 30 minutes.

GENUINE AMERICAN PANCAKES

Sinai Yarus

Measure all dry ingredients into a large mixing bowl and mix. Add all wet ingredients and mix thoroughly using a spoon or whisk until a smooth batter is obtained. Do not use an electric mixer as this makes the pancakes tough. If the batter is too thick, additional milk may be added.

Heat a heavy skillet on the stove (large burner, medium flame) until a drop of water placed in the skillet dances across the surface before evaporating. If necessary, a drop of oil may be applied with a paper towel. Do not put any significant amount of oil or margarine in the skillet. The object is to "bake" the pancakes, not fry them. Pour about 1/3 cup of batter into the skillet.

When persistent bubbles appear (takes about a minute), turn the pancake over and cook for an additional 30-60 seconds. Check that the center is baked before removing from the skillet. If the outside of the pancake is burned and the inside is still liquid, try reducing the heat slightly and/or adding more milk to the batter. The pancakes should be golden brown, thick, and fluffy.

The buttermilk gives a distinctive rich flavor, although regular milk may be used in a pinch. This recipe makes 18-24 pancakes, with a serving size of 3-4, although teenage boys have been known to consume 10 or more. Serve with butter, jam, compote, chocolate spread, butterscotch (Dulce de Lece), or anything else that strikes your fancy.

DRY INGREDIENTS

3 cups flour (preferably 1 cup whole wheat and 2 cups white)

3 tsp baking powder

1 1/2 tsp baking soda

1 tsp salt

3 Tbsp sugar

WET INGREDIENTS

2 cups (500ml) buttermilk (Rivyon)

1 cup milk

3 eggs

1/2 cup oil

2 3/4 cups self-rising flour

2 containers of Eshel (4% fat butter milk)

1 egg

salt

pizza sauce

yellow cheese, grated

toppings, to taste

NO YEAST INSTANT PIZZA

Miriam Weingrover | School Principal

Preheat oven to 180C (350F).

Mix the flour, Eshel, egg, and salt to make the dough. Lightly oil two medium pans. Spread the dough out evenly on the pans. Pour pizza sauce on the dough, sprinkle the cheese on top, and add toppings as desired. Bake until the cheese has melted.

DOUGH

500g (1 lb) flour

100g (4 oz) butter

salt

1/2 cup sour cream

1/2 cup water

1 egg

FILLING

1 large onion

2 cloves garlic

200g (8 oz) butter

2 packages fresh mushrooms

1 cup cream

salt

pepper

nutmeg

150g (6 oz) grated yellow cheese

parve chicken soup powder

MUSHROOM QUICHE

Courtesy of Ma'afe Ne'eman Cafe

DOUGH

Combine all ingredients into soft dough. Roll out and fit into tart pan or 10 individual quiche dishes.

FILLING

Preheat oven to 180C (350F).

Brown onion and garlic over small fire. Add mushrooms and seasoning. Add cream and bring to a boil. Place filling on dough in prepared dishes and top with yellow cheese. Bake for 30 minutes. Note: broccoli, onion, or Brussels sprouts may be substituted for the mushrooms.

ONION QUICHE

Courtesy of "Little Jerusalem" Restaurant
Ticho House

Preheat oven to 180C (350F).

Fry the onions in butter until golden, then cool. Add remaining ingredients and pour into greased and floured baking pan. Bake for 1 hour.

INGREDIENTS

10 large onions, chopped

1 1/2 cups cream

4 eggs

3 Tbsp flour

2 Tbsp breadcrumbs

salt

white pepper

nutmeg

SIMPLE MUSHROOM SOUFFLÉ

Rachel Epstein

Preheat oven to 180C (350F).

Sauté mushrooms and onions. Mix onions and mushrooms with rest of the ingredients. Pour into greased pie dish and bake for 40 to 50 minutes.

INGREDIENTS

2 large onions, chopped

250g (1/2 lb) fresh mushrooms, sliced

250g container (8 oz) low fat cream cheese)

250g container (8 oz) cottage cheese

150g (8 oz) shredded yellow cheese

4 eggs

salt and pepper, to taste

TOBEE'S APPLE KUGEL

Tobee Weisel

Preheat oven to 180C (350F).

In food processor with steel blade, blend flour, sugar, cinnamon, and salt for 20 seconds. Empty flour mixture into large bowl. Blend eggs and oil for 45 seconds until creamy. Add juice to egg and oil mixture, and blend for 15 seconds. Fold egg mixture into flour mixture in large bowl. In food processor with slicing blade, slice apples. Add apples to batter and blend well. Pour into greased 9x13 glass baking pan. Place whole walnuts in rows on top of apple batter.
Bake in oven for 1 hour. Serve warm or cold.

INGREDIENTS

1 1/2 cups flour
1 1/2 cups sugar
1 1/2 tsp cinnamon
scant teaspoon salt
4 eggs
3/4 cup oil
1 cup orange juice
10 green apples, peeled and cored
whole walnuts (optional)

CRANBERRY KUGEL

Tania Cohen

This recipe tastes great as a side dish or as a dessert.

Preheat oven to 180C (350F).

Soften margarine and cream with oats, sugar, flour, and cinnamon. Place half of mixture on bottom of square Pyrex pan to make crust. Place apples on crust. Spoon cranberry sauce on top of apples. Sprinkle remaining crust mixture over apples. Bake for 40 minutes.

INGREDIENTS

100g (1/2 cup) margarine
1 1/2 cups quick oats
1/2 cup brown sugar
1/3 cup flour
pinch of cinnamon
2 apples, peeled and sliced
1 can whole cranberry sauce (optional)

INGREDIENTS

1/2kg (1 lb) fresh pumpkin

1/2 cup mayonnaise

5 eggs

2-3 Tbsp flour

1/4 cup margarine

1/2 cup sugar

PUMPKIN KUGEL

Ettie Davies

Preheat oven to 180C (350F).

Place pumpkin in boiling water and steam until soft enough to be mashed with a fork. Drain and mash. Add everything else. Pour into baking pan. Bake for 45 minutes or until set.

INGREDIENTS

1 cup farfel (ptitim)

1 cup cold water

1 medium carrot, grated

1 medium onion, chopped

1 stalk celery, diced

1/4 green pepper, diced

2 eggs, well beaten

1/4 cup oil

1/2 tsp salt

1/4 tsp pepper

1 Tbsp sugar

1 medium potato, grated

1/2 Tbsp parsley, chopped

INDIVIDUAL VEGETABLE KUGELS

Toby Koren

You actually can cook almost any kugel recipe in muffin tins, but this was my first.

Preheat oven to 190C (375F).

Soak farfel in water for one hour. Pour off excess liquid, but don't press. Sauté onions in oil; add celery, pepper, and carrot until tender crisp. Combine with remaining ingredients. Put 1/4 tsp oil into each muffin tin and heat in oven for 2 minutes. Fill each tin half full with kugel mixture. Bake "muffins" 30 minutes or until brown.

YERUSHALMI KUGEL

Issca Landau

In this recipe the timing between the stages of cooking the noodles and preparing the caramel is crucial.

Cook the noodles according to the instructions on the packet (water, salt and oil). Drain the noodles and wash with a little cold water. Simultaneously melt margarine, sugar, and spices in a pan until a light brown caramel mixture is formed. Make sure that the caramel doesn't stick and burn. Add the hot noodles to the caramel, stirring well, and turn off the heat. Continue stirring until the mixture cools. Add the beaten eggs and pour into a greased baking dish. Cooking time depends on the depth of the dish. The deeper the kugel, the longer the cooking time needed. Cook the kugel at 180C (350F) approximately 45 minutes, or until a dark brown crusty layer is formed on top. Raisins can be added to the mixture before cooking.

INGREDIENTS

500g (17.5 oz) extra thin noodles

1/2 cup margarine

1 cup sugar

4 eggs

1 tsp cinnamon

1 1/2 tsp salt

1 tsp black pepper

Oil for greasing the tin

CHINESE SPAGHETTI

Marilyn Adler

Sauté carrots for 10 minutes, stirring occasionally. Add scallions for additional 5 minutes. Add mushrooms for 5 more minutes. In separate bowl, mix ingredients for sauce. Combine spaghetti, vegetables, and sauce in a pot. Mix well over low heat for 5-10 minutes.

SPAGHETTI

450g (1 lb) spaghetti, cooked, drained, rinsed. Don't overcook.

5 carrots, peeled and grated

6 scallions, sliced

450g (1 lb) fresh mushrooms or 1 large can mushrooms, sliced

SAUCE

1/3 cup soy sauce

2 Tbsp honey or brown sugar

1/2 to 1 tsp ginger

2 tsp crushed garlic

1 tsp sweet chili sauce (optional)

INGREDIENTS

1 cup couscous, uncooked

2 cups broth or water

6 scallions, (green onions), chopped

1 red pepper, chopped

3 cloves garlic, minced

2 tsp canola oil

1 cup mushrooms, sliced

1 cup canned chickpeas, drained and rinsed (optional)

1 medium carrot, chopped

salt and pepper to taste

COUSCOUS AND MUSHROOM CASSEROLE

Sura Avni

In a large saucepan, sauté the green onions, peppers, and garlic in the oil until softened. Add mushrooms and sauté 3-4 minutes longer. Add broth and bring to a boil. Stir in couscous and remaining ingredients. Bring back to a boil, then cover and simmer until all the liquid is absorbed, about 5-10 minutes. Fluff with a fork. Adjust seasonings to taste. If too dry, add a little extra liquid. Serves 6. Freezes well.

INGREDIENTS

6 cups water

250g (8 oz) fine rice noodles

6 Tbsp oil, divided

1 red pepper, cut into thin slices

3 spring onions, cut into 2 cm (3/4 inch) segments

8 button mushrooms, sliced

1/2 cup bean sprouts

salt and freshly ground pepper

2 Tbsp soy sauce

150g (5 oz) fried cashews

2 tsp sesame oil

RICE NOODLES WITH VEGETABLES & CASHEWS

Noami HaCohen | China

Boil water with 1 tsp of salt in a large saucepan. Add the noodles and cook for 5 minutes. Drain and wash well. Transfer to a bowl, add 2 tablespoons oil and mix. Heat remaining oil in frying pan. Add all the vegetables and stir-fry for 4 minutes. Add the noodles and stir-fry for a further 3 minutes. Season with salt and pepper, add soy sauce, and then stir-fry for another minute. Transfer to serving dish. Sprinkle cashew nuts over noodles. Pour small amount of sesame oil over noodles and serve.

NOODLES WITH CABBAGE

Tammy Einhorn

Stir-fry cabbage in a little oil, until soft and browned. Add salt while the cabbage is cooking. Cook noodles according to instructions, drain, and stir into cabbage.

INGREDIENTS

500g (1 lb) medium or large square noodles

1 green cabbage

salt, to taste

oil

PASTA WITH FRESH TOMATO SAUCE

Courtesy of La Guta Restaurant

Boil large pot of water. When water has boiled add some olive oil, salt, and then put in the pasta. Cook for 5-7 minutes, then drain. Put all remaining ingredients in small pot with a small amount of water. Cook until tomato and onion are softened, then transfer to food processor and blend until smooth. Add salt and pepper to taste, and pour over prepared pasta.

INGREDIENTS

500g (1 lb) pasta

4 fresh tomatoes, chopped

1 onion, chopped

1 sprig of thyme

2 cloves garlic

1 Tbsp olive oil

2 Tbsp white wine

1 tsp sugar

TOFU TOMATO SAUCE FOR PASTA

Sigalit Greenbaum

Sauté the onion in a mixture of olive oil and canola oil until light brown. Add the garlic, then the tofu and red and green peppers if using. Sauté until the tofu is light brown. Stir often so the tofu won't stick to the pan. Add the tomato paste, sugar, oregano, salt, and pepper. Cook for 20 minutes over low flame. Serve over pasta.

INGREDIENTS

1 onion, cubed

1 clove garlic, sliced

320g (12 oz) package tofu, cubed

200g (7 oz) tomato paste

red and green peppers, chopped (optional)

1 tsp sugar or to taste

canola and olive oil

salt, pepper, and oregano to taste

DREAMY POTATOES

Toby Koren

INGREDIENTS

500g (1 lb) potatoes, chunked small

2 Tbsp soy sauce, divided

1 tsp brown sugar, packed

1 tsp flour

3 Tbsp peanut oil, divided

1 cup chicken stock or broth

1 tsp sugar

1/4 tsp salt

sesame seeds for garnish

My husband woke up one morning not long ago and said, "I had the most delicious dream – there was some kind of combination of potatoes and soy sauce."
It sounded strange to me, but the potatoes haunted him, and so finally we looked online and found an appropriate recipe. To my surprise, the result was fabulous – we couldn't stop eating them! The only change I'd recommend is to double the recipe, as this calls for only half a kilo of potatoes, which our family of five devoured quickly.

In a bowl, combine potatoes, 1 tablespoon of soy sauce, brown sugar, flour, and 1 tablespoon of the oil. Toss well to coat evenly; refrigerate for at least one hour. Heat remaining oil in a wok over high heat. Add potatoes and stir-fry 2-3 minutes. Add remaining ingredients except sesame seeds. Cover, then lower heat and simmer until potatoes are tender and most liquid is absorbed. Sprinkle with desired amount of sesame seeds and an additional tablespoon of soy sauce, if desired. Serves 4.

MEDITERRANEAN POTATOES

Jay Bailey

INGREDIENTS

3-5 medium-sized potatoes, sliced 1 cm thick

2 Tbsp olive oil

1 medium-sized red onion, sliced

1 cup pitted black olives

3 garlic cloves, chopped

1-2 cups feta cheese, in 1 cm cubes

1 Tbsp basil

1 Tbsp rosemary

Preheat oven to 190C (375F).

Slice potatoes into 1 cm thick slices. Toss potatoes in olive oil to coat and layer in rows in a baking pan, with about 1/4 of each slice resting on the next. Sprinkle with salt and pepper and bake for about 30 minutes or until they begin to brown lightly and soften. Remove pan from oven.

Drain black olives and smash with the side of a knife. Sprinkle the red onion, olives, garlic, and cheese evenly over the potatoes, and sprinkle with rosemary and basil, making sure that ingredients also slip down in between the layers. Return to oven and bake until cheese is lightly but evenly browned, but before any of the topping has dried out and shrunken significantly. Serve warm or refrigerate and reheat.

EASY PARVE SCALLOPED POTATOES

Joy Gris

Preheat oven to 180C (350F).

Boil potatoes until just tender. Reserve 1 cup of the water for later. Sauté onions in margarine until translucent. Mix 1 cup water from potatoes with onions. Add mayonnaise and spices. Place one layer of potatoes in casserole dish.Pour layer of sauce over. Repeat layer of potatoes and then a layer of sauce. Sprinkle top with paprika. Bake for 45 minutes or until brown on top.

INGREDIENTS

7-8 potatoes, peeled and sliced thin

2 large onions, chopped

3 Tbsp margarine

3 heaping Tbsp mayonnaise

1 tsp garlic powder

1 tsp onion powder

1 tsp salt

paprika

1 cup water reserved from boiled potatoes

BAKED SWEET POTATO STICKS

Sue Epstein   Author of "Budget Cooking-Elegant Dining" and "Simply Delicious"

These yummy sticks are best eaten at room temperature. A great substitute for French Fries.

Preheat oven to 200C (400F).

Lightly grease a baking sheet. In a large bowl, mix olive oil and paprika. Add potato sticks, and stir by hand to coat. Place on the prepared baking sheet. Bake 40 minutes in the preheated oven.

INGREDIENTS

1 Tbsp olive oil

1/2 tsp paprika

8 sweet potatoes, sliced lengthwise into quarters

COLUMN A:

beef broth (pareve or not)

chicken broth (pareve or not)

mushroom broth

vegetable broth

COLUMN B:

parsley

thyme

basil

mint

COLUMN C:

red bell pepper and garlic, chopped and sautéed

asparagus, sliced, and steamed

carrots, raisins, and toasted pine nuts

celery and mushrooms, sliced and sautéed

COLUMN D:

cucumber

red onion, chopped

scallions, sliced

feta cheese, crumbled

256 WAYS TO COOK RICE

Sue Epstein   author of "Budget Cooking-Elegant Dining" and "Simply Delicious"

Cook rice for 4 servings in a liquid from Column A, stir in an herb (1 tablespoon chopped, fresh or 1 tsp dried) from Column B, add a choice from Column C and top with an ingredient from Column D.

INGREDIENTS

1 can sliced mushrooms, reserve liquid

1 cup uncooked rice

2 Tbsp oil

2 Tbsp soy sauce

2 Tbsp onion soup powder

2 cups liquid (liquid from canned mushrooms plus water)

VERY EASY BAKED RICE

Barbara Asch

Preheat oven to 180C (350F).

Mix mushrooms and rice together in a baking pan. Add other ingredients and mix well. Add liquid. Cover and cook for 1 1/2 hours.

SPICY RICE, BEAN, ANDLENTIL CASSEROLE

Aliza Beinhaker

Sauté onion and garlic. Add stock, rice, lentils, basil, and chili powder. Bring to a boil and then reduce heat to low. Cook 30-40 minutes until tender. Stir in beans, corn, and salsa, and cook for 5 more minutes.

INGREDIENTS

2 tsp oil

2 tsp garlic, chopped

1 large onion, chopped

3 3/4 cups water

2 Tbsp chicken soup powder

3/4 cup brown rice

1/2 cup lentils

1 tsp dried basil

3/4 tsp chili powder

1 can kidney beans

1 cup corn

1 cup salsa

BROCCOLI AND WHITE RICE CASSEROLE

Tzippy Gutman

Preheat oven to 180C (350F).

In a casserole dish, mix broccoli, rice, salt, oil, and water. Cook in microwave for 5 minutes on high until water is almost absorbed. Beat the egg in a small dish, add to rice mixture and mix quickly with a fork. Sprinkle paprika on top. Bake for 45 minutes.

INGREDIENTS

1 bunch broccoli cut into 2 cm (3/4 inch) pieces

2 cups raw white rice

1 tsp salt

2 Tbsp olive oil

3 1/2 cups water

1 egg

paprika

GRAPE LEAVES

50 vine leaves

STUFFING

3 cups rice, rinsed 3 times

2 Tbsp oil

1 large onion

1 large tomato

3 cloves of garlic

salt

black pepper

paprika

STOCK

citric acid

1/2 cup of oil

water to cover

STUFFED GRAPE LEAVES

Hannah Ido   Iraq

VINE LEAVES

They can be picked here in Efrat in season. Pour boiling water on them and let stand until they change colour. Drain and store in the freezer in packets of 50.

STUFFING

Blend onion, tomato, and garlic in food processor. Add oil and spices. Open vine leaves and place one teaspoon rice filling near bottom. Fold sides inwards, roll and seal.

STOCK

Arrange vine-rolls tightly on the bottom of an oiled pot. Layer the rest of the leaves on top. Cover with water, not too much, or the filling will go soggy!Add citric acid and oil. Bring to a boil. Reduce heat, cook until most of the liquid is absorbed, then turn off flame. Press the leaves down occasionally with the back of a spoon during cooking. Leave pot closed for another 10 minutes or so. If the rolls are done properly, you should be able to turn the whole pot upside down onto a plate. If this doesn't work, take each one out carefully with a fork to prevent tearing!

INGREDIENTS

1 cup green lentils

1 1/2 cups rice

2 1/4 cups water

3 large onions

oil for frying

salt and pepper

MAJADRA

Hazel Vahav | Persia

Cover lentils with water and cook lentils for 1/2 hour. Drain lentils and set aside. Cook rice, salt, and water on low flame for 1/2 hour or until the water has been absorbed. Sauté the onion until golden brown and put on top of cooked rice. Stab the rice with a knife so that the oil is absorbed into the rice mixture.

MEXICAN RICE

David Cohen

In heavy skillet, sauté onion, peppers, and tomatoes in oil until soft. Stir in rice and tomato sauce. Add water and salt. Bring to boil slowly. Cover and cook on low flame for 20 minutes or until all water is absorbed.

INGREDIENTS

2/3 cup onion, chopped

1 cup green pepper, chopped

1 chili pepper, optional

1 cup fresh tomatoes, chopped

3 Tbsp oil

1 cup rice

1 small can of tomato sauce

2 tsp salt

2 cups of water

BROWN RICE & SPINACH

Shoshana Rotkoff

Sauté onion and rice in olive oil, stirring occasionally, for ten minutes. Add boiling water and salt, cover and cook on low flame for ten minutes. If using fresh spinach, wash well and slice. Add spinach to rice, mix and cover. Continue cooking on low flame until the rice is tender, stirring occasionally.

INGREDIENTS

1 cup brown rice

400 - 500g (12-16 oz) frozen spinach

1 medium onion, chopped

1/3 cup olive oil

2 cups boiling water

1 1/2 tsp salt

PEPPERS

6 red peppers

FILLING

2 cups whole
grain rice

2-3 carrots and
zucchini, grated

1 onion, diced and
sautéed

2 Tbsp tomato paste

SAUCE

1 onion, diced and
fried

tomato paste

salt

bay leaves

Peppers

RICE AND VEGETABLES STUFFED PEPPERS

Emanuel and Rachel Shreiber

Cut the tops off the peppers and take out the seeds.
Keep the caps.

FILLING

In a bowl mix the rice, fried onion, grated vegetables,
salt, and tomato paste. Fill the peppers half-way with
the rice mixture and place the "cap" on top.

SAUCE

In a pot, mix the tomato paste, bay leaves, salt, and fried
onion. Stand the stuffed peppers in the pot. Add water
until half way up the peppers and cook until they are
soft. Place the peppers in a serving bowl and drizzle a
small amount of gravy over the top.

INGREDIENTS

2 cups uncooked rice

1 large onion, diced

2 carrots, thinly sliced

3 potatoes, diced

1/2 can corn, drained

1/2 can peas, drained
(optional)

3 boneless chicken
breasts, cut into small
pieces

2 Tbsp chicken soup
powder

3 Tbsp oil

Salt, pepper, garlic
powder to taste

Dash of cumin (optional)

SHERONI'S RICE

Amy Schlakman

*My friend Sheroni, from Sri Lanka, gave me this recipe.
It is great for using leftover rice and chicken.*

Cook rice as directed with chicken soup mix. Sauté
chicken in oil until no longer pink. Add potatoes, onions,
and carrots and sauté until soft. Add corn, peas, and rice
and mix over medium to low heat for 5 minutes. Add
salt, pepper, garlic, and cumin to taste.

TOFU AND TAHINA AND RICE CASSEROLE

Tamar Shreiger

For your information, "shoyu" soy sauce contains wheat while "tamari" soy sauce does not.

CASSEROLE

Mix the broccoli and the cooked rice. Fry the onion and add to the rice and broccoli.

SAUCE

In a food processor, mix the tofu, tehina, salt, pepper, lemon juice, soy sauce, and mustard. More tehina, lemon juice, or soy sauce may be added to improve taste. Add the mixture to the rice before serving. The casserole may be baked before serving or just heated through.

CASSEROLE

3 cups cooked rice

oil

1 medium onion, chopped

1 cup steamed broccoli, chopped

SAUCE

1 package tofu, crumbled

2 Tbsp raw tehina

1/2 tsp salt

black pepper

1 tsp soy sauce

1 tsp mustard

1 tsp lemon juice

1 cup soy milk or water

BAKED BARLEY WITH SAUTÉED VEGETABLES

Jay Bailey

Preheat oven to 190C (375F).

Sauté the vegetables in olive oil for about 5 minutes, or just until they start to soften and change color. Rinse the barley and add it to the vegetables until everything starts to brown. The barley will get lightly toasted and absorb some of the liquid/oil. Pour the chicken stock (or mix the powder and water) into a 9x13 Pyrex baking pan and dump the sautéd mixture into it. Mix completely, and bake uncovered for 60-75 minutes. The barley will absorb the liquid, and the whole thing will brown lightly on top.

INGREDIENTS

3 peppers, in at least 2 colors, chopped

1 medium onion, chopped

1 cup cabbage, chopped

3 Tbsp olive oil

salt and pepper

1 1/2 cups barley

3 cups chicken stock – the real thing or soup powder in water

INGREDIENTS

2/3 cup barley

2 onions, chopped

1 cup cauliflower, cut small

1 cup mushrooms, chopped

1 cup carrots, finely shredded

3 cups vegetable stock, divided

1/4 tsp garlic powder

BARLEY VEGETABLE CASSEROLE

Ettie Davies

Preheat oven to 180C (350F).

Place barley and 1/2 cup stock in skillet over medium heat. Cook 2-3 minutes, stirring frequently, until lightly browned. Transfer to lightly greased casserole dish. Sauté onions 5 minutes in same skillet, stirring frequently. Combine onions with remaining vegetables and add to casserole. Stir in remaining 2 1/2 cups vegetable stock and garlic powder. Mix well. Cover and bake 1 1/4 hours. Stir several times while baking. Bake until barley is tender and most of the liquid has been absorbed. Let stand 5 minutes. Then mix again and serve.

INGREDIENTS

1 small red cabbage, sliced medium-thin

1 onion, sliced medium-thin

1/4 cup brown sugar

1 Tbsp salt

1 cup red wine (either dry or sweet; both work)

1 cup red wine vinegar

50g (1/4 cup) butter or margarine, or canola oil (see note)

1 apple, peeled, cored, and diced

1/4 cup hot water

1/8 tsp cloves

1/4 tsp cinnamon

BRAISED RED CABBAGE

Dena Landau

Mix sliced cabbage with sugar, salt, and vinegar in a large bowl and marinate 15 minutes. Melt butter in 5-quart pot over medium heat, then add onion and sauté 5 minutes or until transparent. Add apple and sauté 5 more minutes. Add cabbage mixture to pot, add wine, and bring to a boil; reduce heat. Combine hot water, cloves, and cinnamon. Add to cabbage mixture. Cover and simmer 1 hour or until tender and moisture has cooked away. Serve immediately, or later at room temperature.

Note – if you make this dairy, use butter instead of margarine. If you plan on serving it at room temperature, use oil so that it doesn't solidify.

STUFFED CABBAGE

Shellie Davis

My mom makes this every Succot. The whole house smells yummy and we all wait anxiously to eat them!

Put cabbage in the microwave for 10 minutes. Separate leaves and roll the meat in. Put in a large pot, layering until all of the meat is used. Pour marinara sauce and honey on top. Cook on low flame for 1 1/2 hours covered. This freezes well and is delicious!

INGREDIENTS

3 heads cabbage

1kg (2 lbs) chopped meat

1 jar (737g /26 oz) marinara sauce

1/2 cup honey

CAULIFLOWER WITH BREADCRUMBS

Tammi Einhorn

Cook cauliflower until slightly softened. Strain in cold water to stop cooking process. Fry breadcrumbs in oil and salt for a couple of minutes, stir constantly. Add the cauliflower, and without using a spoon, stir fry by moving pan on stove top.

INGREDIENTS

3 cauliflowers, medium sized

1 cup flavored bread crumbs, good quality

oil for frying

dash of salt

3-4 large onions, sliced

3 hard boiled eggs

1 can garden peas

100g (3 1/2 oz) walnuts

spices

VEGETARIAN CHOPPED LIVER

Matya Tor-Paz

Fry onions in a small amount of oil until brown. Grind the walnuts well in a food processor. Add the peas, eggs, fried onions, and spices. Process to desired consistency.

PASTRY

2 cups flour

1/2 tsp salt

2/3 cup frozen margarine

100ml (3 fl oz) water

FILLING

1 large eggplant, peeled and diced

1 large onion, diced

oil for frying

4 Tbsp mushroom soup mix

1 can of mushrooms, with liquid

MUSHROOM PIE

Efrat Matamim Catering | Joni Liwerant | 9931918.

PASTRY

Preheat oven to 180C (350F).

Blend dry ingredients in the food processor for 12 seconds or until crumbly. Add the water and mix another 6 seconds or until the dough forms a ball. Roll out approximately half the pastry into a 9x13 pan. Set aside. Keep the rest of the pastry to cover the pie.

FILLING

Sauté the onion until they begin to brown. Add eggplant to the onion mixture and sauté until everything is browned and soft. Add the soup powder and then the mushrooms with the liquid. Continue cooking for a few more minutes. Let cool. Pour the mixture on the base. Spread evenly. Roll out the remaining pastry. Cover the pie. Brush with egg. Sprinkle with sesame seeds. Bake for 1 hour.

SAVORY PLAIT

Adiva Beigel | England

I learned how to make this at school in England.

Preheat oven to 180C (350F).

Finely chop all the vegetables. The list of vegetables is a recommendation and can be varied. Roll the pastry out thinly into a rectangle. Mark 2 lines in the length dividing the rectangle into three. Place the vegetables along the centre. Cut the outer sections of the pastry into strips in the width. The pastry will look like two combs on either side of the filling. Plait the strips one over the other, over the filling. Bake for 20 minutes.

INGREDIENTS

1 sheet puff pastry

onion, finely chopped

red pepper, finely chopped

tomato, finely chopped

zucchini, finely chopped

tuna, optional

VEGGIE "MEAT" BALLS IN TOMATO AND BELL PEPPER SAUCE

Elisheva Hershler

"MEAT" BALLS
Defrost the chopped "meat." Soak the bread, squeeze out the water, and crush into crumbs. Mix all the ingredients and form into balls.

SAUCE
Heat the oil, red pepper, and thyme in a pot. Add the meatballs and cook for 2-3 minutes. Add the crushed tomatoes and season with salt and pepper. There is no need to stir. Gently bring to a boil and simmer for an hour. Add water if the sauce evaporates.

"MEAT" BALLS

500g (1 lb) vegetarian chopped "meat"

1 onion, diced

1 garlic clove, crushed

1 slice stale bread

1 egg

1/2 tsp cumin or meatball spice

1/2 cup breadcrumbs

SAUCE

1 Tbsp olive oil

4 sprigs fresh thyme

1/2 red pepper, sliced into strips

3 ripe tomatoes, crushed

salt and pepper

INGREDIENTS

2 packages (320g / 10 oz each) extra-firm tofu, sliced

3 medium onions, chopped

1 large or 2 small green peppers, chopped

500g (1 lb) mushrooms, sliced

oil for frying

1 large jar (25 oz) marinara sauce

1 560g (15.5 oz) can tomato sauce

oregano

salt

TOFU CACCIATORE

Sue Kaplan | Chicago

Slice the tofu about the size of dominoes. Put 1/4 inch of oil into a large frying pan. Fry the tofu slices in batches on both sides until lightly browned, and remove each batch to drain on paper towels when done. This usually takes 2-3 batches of frying. Discard most of the oil, but leave just enough to sauté the onions, peppers, and mushrooms. When onions are tender, add all remaining ingredients, including fried tofu slices. Simmer together an additional 5 minutes. Serve over rice.

INGREDIENTS

1kg (2 lb) carrots and sweet potato, cubed

6 Tbsp olive oil

1 Tbsp fresh rosemary leaves

6 Tbsp balsamic vinegar

2 Tbsp brown sugar

salt and pepper

BAKED ROOT VEGETABLES

Liraz Infeld

Preheat the oven to 220C (425F).

Heat the oil in a Pyrex dish that can also go on the stovetop. Add all the ingredients to the Pyrex dish and mix. Cook on the stovetop for 15 minutes and place in the oven for 60 minutes. Check the vegetables occasionally so they don't dry out, and mix them so the gravy covers them. If the gravy dries out, add some water or white wine.

ROASTED VEGETABLES

Sharon Meisels

Preheat the oven to 180C (350F).

Line a baking tray with aluminium foil and spray with olive oil. Mix the vegetables with olive oil and spread over the tray. Bake for around 40 minutes, stirring 2-3 times. The vegetables should be slightly firm and not overcooked. Remove from heat and put into a bowl to cool to which you add the tablespoon of vinegar. This dish is good eaten hot or cold and can be served in a bowl or on a flat serving dish.

INGREDIENTS

4 zucchinis, sliced

1 eggplant, sliced (sprinkle with salt to drain off the bitter juices for 30 minutes, rinse in cold water and leave to drain)

12 cherry tomatoes, cut in half

2-3 peppers, sliced (use different colours)

6 cloves of garlic, sliced

rosemary, fresh or dry

2-3 Tbsp olive oil

1 Tbsp Balsamic vinegar

WHEAT BERRY STEW (HARISA)

Chagit Houminer | Libya

A traditional wheat dish from the Jews of Tripoli, Libya.

Soak the wheat berries in water overnight. Fry the onions in oil until golden and add the garlic, sweet paprika, tomato paste, and a small amount of water. Bring to a boil and simmer for 20 minutes. Add the wheat berries, eggs, and salt. Add enough water to cover the wheat berries and eggs. Cook for 20 minutes more and put on the Shabbat hot plate. Leave overnight and serve in the morning.

INGREDIENTS

1 cup wheat berries

1 onion, chopped

garlic

2 Tbsp sweet paprika

2 Tbsp tomato paste

a little water

1 Tbsp salt

2-3 whole eggs

CHALLAH

Ann Goodman

Preheat the oven to 180C (350F).

Add salt with the flour. You can add up to another 1/2 kg flour if needed. Knead dough. Let it rest until doubled and then punch down.

Take challah with a bracha.

Form into loaves and then brush with beaten eggs. Sprinkle with sesame seeds and bake 30-35 minutes until bottom sounds hollow when tapped.

INGREDIENTS

100g (3 1/2 oz) fresh yeast or 6-7 Tbsp instant dry active yeast

5 cups lukewarm water

2 cups sugar

1 cup oil

3 eggs

3 Tbsp salt

2 1/2kg (5 lb) flour

sesame seeds, optional

WHOLE WHEAT CHALLAH

Magash HaKesef Catering

Preheat the oven to 180C (350F).

Dissolve yeast in 1/2 cup water together with 4 tablespoons of honey. Add half the amount of flour. Add honey, eggs, and half the oil. Knead in a mixer until smooth. Cover with a damp cloth and let rise for 30 minutes. Add remaining water, flour, oil, and salt. Knead until smooth and spongy and a little moist. Let rise a second time for 45 minutes. Divide the dough in 3 and shape into Challas. Place on floured tray and let rise a further 30 minutes. Bake for 15-30 minutes. Tap the bread and listen for a hollow sound to know that it's done. Be sure not to overbake, better slightly moist than dry!

INGREDIENTS

50g (2 oz) fresh yeast

1/2 cup tepid water

1 Tbsp honey

1kg (2 lb) whole wheat flour

1 1/2 cups tepid water

1/2 cup olive oil

1/2 cup honey

1 1/2 Tbsp salt

3 eggs, at room temperature

YEMENITE JAHNUN

Daniel Ofri | Yemen

Daniel Ofri | Yemen

INGREDIENTS

500g (1 lb) whole wheat flour

warm water, as needed

a pinch of salt

200g (1/2 lb) margarine, softened

50g (1 1/2 oz) fresh yeast

Place all the ingredients in a bowl with a little margarine and knead until a uniform dough has formed. Roll out the dough and spread a layer of margarine. Fold the dough and repeat the process 4 times to created a layered dough. After spreading the last layer of margarine roll the dough out again and slice into wide strips. Roll each strip and place the rolls in a pan next to each other. Spread a layer of margarine under each layer of rolled dough. Place the pan in an oven overnight, at a very low temperature.

Serving suggestion: hard boiled egg, grated tomato, or hot sauce.

CHEESECAKE

Sigalit Greenbaum

CRUST

2 cups graham cracker crumbs

100g (1/2 cup) soft butter

FILLING

625g containers (22 oz) 5% fat cream cheese

200ml container (7/8 cup) sour cream

200ml container (7/8 cup) Leben/buttermilk

1 Tbsp vanilla

6 heaped Tbsp flour

6 eggs, separated

1 1/2 cups sugar, divided

TOPPING

1 cup whipping cream

1 cup cold milk

1/2 package instant vanilla pudding

CRUST

Preheat oven to 180C (350F). Mix crumbs with butter. Pat into a cheesecake pan.

FILLING

Beat the egg yolks with 1 cup sugar until creamy. Add everything except the egg whites and the remaining 1/2 cup sugar. Beat the whites with the 1/2 cup sugar until stiff. Fold whites into cheese mixture. Pour into prepared pan and bake until light brown. Turn off the oven and leave the cake in the oven another 20 minutes after it's done. Cool.

TOPPING

Combine topping ingredients and pour over cake when the cake is completely cooled.

NO BAKE CHEESECAKE

Café Rimon   Jerusalem

Beat together cheese, egg yolks, sugar, vanilla sugar, and lemon rind. Dissolve gelatin in 1/2 cup of boiling water, and add to mixture. Whip cream and fold into cheese mixture. Line a 9 inch round pan with prepared cake layer. Cover with cheese mixture and freeze over night. Spread blueberry filling over cake and keep refrigerated.

INGREDIENTS

500g (1 lb) 5% cream cheese

3 egg yolks

1 Tbsp gelatin

2 tsp vanilla-sugar

rind of one lemon

1 cup heavy cream

1 can blueberry pie-filling

pre-baked cake layer

NAOMI'S EASY CHEESECAKE

Felicity Aziz

BASE
Preheat oven to 160C (325F).

Crumble the biscuits (easier in a paper bag). Add the margarine, mix together, place in pie dish forming a base of about 5 mm (1/4 inch) high. Bake in the oven for 15 minutes.

FILLING
Preheat oven to 200C (400F).

In an electric mixer add the cheese and yogurt and the sugar in small amounts each time. Add all the flour. Add the egg yolks and the vanilla essence to the mixture and place the egg whites in a separate bowl. Beat the egg whites until stiff, then fold them into the cheese mixture using a wooden spoon. Pour the mixture onto the pre-baked base and bake for 45 minutes. Leave to cool for 15 minutes.

TOPPING
Preheat oven to 90C (200F).

Combine the yogurt, sugar, and vanilla essence. Place on the cooled cake. Place in oven for 20 minutes.

BASE

200 g (7 oz) petite buerre biscuits

1/4 cup soft margarine

FILLING

500g (16 oz) 5% fat cream cheese

7/8 cup 1.5% fat yogurt

1/2 cup sugar

2 Tbsp flour

2 eggs, separated

1 tsp vanilla essence

TOPPING

1 1/3 cups yogurt

1 Tbsp sugar

1 tsp vanilla essence

CRUST

120g (4 oz) chocolate-flavored petit-beurre biscuits, crumbled

3/8 cup butter, melted

1/4 cup white sugar (optional)

FILLING

680g (24 oz) containers cream cheese, at least 9% fat

1 cup sugar

1/4 cup flour

2 tsp vanilla

6 eggs

1 cup sour cream

170g (6 oz) semi-sweet chocolate chips, melted

MOM'S MARBLE CHEESECAKE

Suzie Friedman

Preheat oven to 200C (400F).

CRUST

Combine melted butter, mashed biscuits, and sugar. Press into a 9-inch spring form pan. Bakefor 10 minutes.

FILLING

Beat cream cheese and sugar at medium speed. Blend in flour and vanilla. Add eggs. Blend in sour cream. Melt chocolate in a double-boiler pot or a microwave oven. Be careful not to let it burn. Stir often. Take off 1 3/4 cups of the cheese batter and blend it with the melted chocolate. Pour the white batter into the crust. Add spoonfuls of the chocolate batter into the white batter and marbleize by pulling a knife through the batter. Put the cake into oven, and immediately turn down the oven to 150C (300F). Bake for 1 hour. Let the cake cool in the oven with the oven door open. (Hopefully this will reduce the likelihood of the cake cracking!)

INGREDIENTS

4 eggs, separated

1 cup sugar

500g (1 lb) low fat cream cheese

3 scant Tbsp potato starch

1/2 bag vanilla flavour instant pudding

1/2 cup buttermilk (Eshel)

ground almonds

PESACH CHEESE CAKE

Esti Seville

Preheat oven to 180C (350F).

Sprinkle pan with ground almonds. Whip egg whites with 1/2 cup of sugar until stiff and set aside. Whip yolks with remaining half cup of sugar and gradually add the rest of the ingredients. Gently fold in the egg whites. Bake for 1 hour.

REFRIDGERATOR CHEESE CAKE

Naomi Fruedenberger

CRUST

Mix cookie crumbs with melted butter. Add sugar. Pour half the cookie crumbs on the bottom of the baking pan.

FILLING:

Mix filling ingredients well. Pour onto crumb crust. Spoon remaining crumbs on top. Refrigerate over night.

CRUST

2 cups cookie crumbs, Petit Buerre

1/4 cup butter, melted

3 Tbsp sugar

FILLING

500g (2 lb) of 5% or 9% fat cream cheese

1 container (3/4 cup) sour cream

1/2 cup sugar

1 Tbsp vanilla sugar

1 box instant vanilla pudding

CHOCOLATE CAKE WITH CHOCOLATE ICING

Avigayil Rachamim

CAKE

Preheat oven to 150C (300F).

Mix all dry ingredients together. Except for the boiling water, add wet ingredients and mix well. Now add the water and blend. Pour into well greased 26 cm (12 inch) pan. Bake for 30-40 minutes or until the crust is dry.

ICING

Melt chocolate and add flavorings. Spread on cake and decorate with sprinkles.

CAKE

2 cups self-rising flour

1 1/2 cups sugar

1 tsp baking soda

pinch of salt

3 heaping Tbsp cocoa

1/2 cup oil

3/4 cup water

2 eggs

3/4 cup boiling water

ICING

100g (4 oz) bittersweet chocolate

rum flavoring

vanilla flavoring

CAKE

120g (1/2 cup +
2 Tbsp) butter

120g (1/2 cup +
2 Tbsp) sugar

60g (2 oz) potato flour

4 eggs, separated

180 g (6 oz) dark
chocolate

1 tsp baking powder

1/2 tsp vanilla
essence

ICING

60g (1/4 cup +
1 Tbsp) butter

120g (4 oz) rich dark
chocolate

brandy to taste

nuts, optional

JULIET'S PESACH CHOCOLATE CAKE

Hazel Vahav

CAKE

Preheat oven to 180C (350F).

Melt butter in large pan. Add broken chocolate and
stir until melted. Remove from heat and add sugar,
egg yolks, vanilla essence, baking powder, and potato
flour. Fold in stiffly beaten egg whites. Bake for 35-40
minutes. Leave on cooling rack to cool.

ICING

Melt chocolate and butter over hot water or in
microwave. Add brandy. Smooth over sides and top with
flat cake knife. Decorate with nuts (optional).

CAKE

1 1/2 cup oil

2 cups sugar

4 eggs

1 cup cocoa

1 1/3 cup flour

1 tsp baking powder

1 tsp vanilla

TOPPING

1/2 cup petit beurre
or graham cracker
crumbs

1/2 cup chopped
walnuts

1/2 cup chocolate
chips

2 Tbsp melted
margarine

CRUNCHY CRUMB TOPPING CHOCOLATE CAKE

Gail Ehrlich (Gili's Goodies)

Preheat oven to 180C (350F).

Mix cake ingredients together and pour into a greased
9x13 pan.

Mix topping ingredients together and pour over
unbaked cake. Bake for 40 minutes.

MELTED CHOCOLATE CUPCAKES

Leticia Baer | France

Preheat oven to 260C (500F).

Melt 100g of chocolate and then add the butter. Mix the eggs, sugar, and flour in a bowl. Add the melted chocolate and mix. Pour 1/3 of the mixture into 4 depressions of a muffin pan. Place two cubes of chocolate on the batter and then pour the rest of the batter on top. Bake for 10 minutes. Serve warm.

INGREDIENTS

100g (3 1/2 oz) semi sweet chocolate, melted

8 small cubes of chocolate, whole

3 eggs

80g (1/3 cup and 1 Tbsp) sugar

50g (1 1/2 oz) butter

1 Tbsp flour

CHOCOLATE MOUSSE CAKE

Barbara Lang

Preheat oven to 180C (350F).

Melt chocolate and margarine together. Beat egg whites until stiff. Beat together egg yolks and sugar, and then mix in the melted chocolate and liqueur. Fold in beaten egg whites. Pour half the mixture into a 26 cm springform pan. Bake for 20 minutes (no more). After the cake has cooled and fallen, pour the rest of the mousse on top. Put into freezer and take out 20-30 minutes before serving.

INGREDIENTS

8 eggs, separated

100g (1/2 cup) margarine

300g (10 oz) bitter-sweet chocolate

1/2 cup sugar

1 Tbsp liqueur

EASY CHOCOLATE MOUSSE CAKE

Vered Sheinbach

INGREDIENTS

200g (7 oz) bittersweet chocolate, broken into squares

3 Tbsp cocoa

1/4 cup milk substitute

200g (1 cup) margarine

8 eggs, separated

1/2 - 3/4 cup sugar

Preheat oven to 180C (350F).

Melt the chocolate, margarine, milk substitute, and cocoa in a double pot. Take the pot off the stove and cool. Beat the egg yolks and add them to the chocolate. Beat the egg whites with the sugar until stiff and fold them into the chocolate. Divide the batter in half. Pour half the batter into a greased, round 26-28 cm (12 inch) pan. Bake for 30-40 minutes. Check the cake with a toothpick and when done, remove from oven. After completely cooled, pour the reserved mousse on top. In order to make a black and white mousse cake beat non-dairy whipping with 1-2 teaspoons of sugar and spread on top of mousse.

COCOA APPLE CAKE

Elaine Beychok

INGREDIENTS

3 eggs

2 cups sugar

200g (1 cup) margarine

1/2 cup water

2 1/2 cups flour

2 Tbsp cocoa

1 tsp baking soda

1 tsp cinnamon

1 cup finely chopped walnuts

2 cups grated apples

1 Tbsp vanilla

1 cup chocolate chips

Preheat oven to 160C (325 F).

Cream eggs, sugar, margarine, and water until fluffy. Sift together flour, cocoa, baking soda, and cinnamon. Add to creamed mixture and mix well. Fold in walnuts, apples, vanilla, and chocolate chips. Mix until distributed evenly. Spoon into greased, floured 10 inch loose-bottom tube pan or bundt pan. Bake 60-70 minutes until cake tests done. Serves 12.

COCOA SQUARES

Janet Kupietzky

Preheat oven to 180C (350F).

Put oil, cocoa, eggs, sugar, and remaining dry ingredients in bowl. Mix until well blended. Gradually add the cold water and vanilla. Beat until blended. Pour into ungreased pan (11 x 17, 9 x 13, or two square or round pans). Sprinkle with chocolate bits. (I find it bakes better when divided into two smaller pans.)

Bake for 30-40 minutes (varies depending on the size of the pan). Cool in pan. This cake freezes well.

INGREDIENTS

7/8 cup oil

3/4 cup cocoa

2 eggs

2 cups of sugar

2 1/2 cups of flour, mixed with

1 tsp baking soda and 1 tsp salt

1 1/2 cups cold water

1 tsp vanilla

1 cup chocolate bits (chips)

CREAM CRUMB CAKE

Matia Tur-Paz

Preheat oven to 180C (350F).

Melt margarine and add all remaining base ingredients. Into greased pan, pour 2/3 of the base pastry and pour remaining 1/3 into separate greased pan. Bake until firm. Mix all filling ingredients and pour onto 2/3 baked pastry. Crumble the 1/3 baked pastry and sprinkle on top of filling. Refrigerate until served.

BASE

200g (1 cup) margarine

2 eggs

1/2 cup sugar

350g (12 oz) self-rising flour

FILLING

200g (1 cup) margarine

1 egg

3 cups heavy cream

1 cup sugar

1 package vanilla-sugar

1 cup flour

200g (1 cup) cold margarine, cut in pieces

1/2 cup brown sugar, packed

1/2 tsp cinnamon

CAKE

2 eggs

1 cup sugar

1 tsp vanilla

1/2 cup oil

3/4 cup orange or apple juice

2 cups flour

3 tsp baking powder

1/2 tsp salt

CRUMB CAKE

Ilana Nurkin

CRUMB TOPPING

Process ingredients in food processor for 8-10 seconds until well blended. Set aside

CAKE

Preheat oven to 150C (325F).

Process eggs with sugar and vanilla for 1 minute in food processor. Add oil and process for 1 minute longer. While machine is running, add juice through feed tube and process for 3 seconds. Add dry ingredients. Process with 3-4 quick on/off turns, just until flour disappears. Pour into greased 9 inch square or 7x11 oblong baking pan. Top with crumb topping and bake for 40-50 minutes, until cake tests done.

FILLING

4 cooking apples, peeled and sliced

4 pears, peeled and sliced

2 Tbsp corn flour

1/2 tsp ground nutmeg

1/2 tsp ground cloves

1/2 tsp cinnamon

1/2 cup brown sugar

1 1/2 Tbsp lemon juice

grated rind of 1 lemon

2 tsp vanilla essence

2 1/2 Tbsp butter, melted and cooled

CRUMBLE BASE

1/3 cup brown sugar

75 g (2 1/2 oz) cold butter cut into cubes

pinch of salt

3/4 cup flour

2 tsp grated lemon rind

HOT APPLE & PEAR CAKE

Naomi HaCohen

FILLING

Preheat oven to 190C (375F).

Place apples and pears in large bowl. In a small bowl mix all dry ingredients. Add lemon juice and rind, vanilla essence and melted butter, and mix. Add the butter mixture to the fruit and mix well.

CRUMBLE BASE

Place all ingredients in electric mixer bowl and, using short pulses, form crumb mixture the size of small peas. Place fruit and juices into 25x25 cm Pyrex dish (10x10 inches). Spread crumb mixture over the fruit evenly. Bake for 45 minutes until the crumb topping turns golden and the fruit is soft when tested with a sharp knife. Serve the cake hot with cream or vanilla ice cream with a sprinkle of cinnamon.

MOM'S BANANA CAKE

Daphna Pearl

This is a double recipe – makes two bundt pans

Preheat oven to 180C (350F).

Mix all ingredients in a mixer at medium speed. Pour into 2 bundt pans. Bake for 45 minutes.

INGREDIENTS

6 eggs

3 cups sugar

1 1/2 cups oil

3/4 cup water

1 1/2 tsp vanilla

4 cups flour

3 tsp baking powder

1 1/2 tsp baking soda

9 mushy bananas, mashed

CARROT ORANGE CAKE

Tzippy Grunstein

Preheat oven to 150C (300F).

Mix dry ingredients and nuts. Add eggs and oil and mix. Process the orange in food processor. Add carrots and orange to flour mixture. Mix 3 minutes. Pour into lightly greased tube pan or 2 loaf pans. Bake for 50-60 minutes.

INGREDIENTS

2 cups flour

2 cups sugar

2 cups carrots, grated

2 tsp cinnamon

2 tsp nutmeg

1 large orange, cut in quarters

1 tsp salt (optional)

1/2 cup nuts (optional)

4 eggs

1/4 cup oil

DATE NUT BREAD

Amy Schlakman

My grandmother, Blanch Winetsky, was famous for this lowfat recipe. Try a slice with cream cheese on top!

Preheat oven to 180C (350F).

Cut dates, add baking soda, and pour boiling water over this combination. Cover and allow to cool. Cream butter, sugar, and eggs. Add dates alternately with flour, a little at a time. Add nuts. Bake in greased loaf pan for about 1 hour.

INGREDIENTS

250g (1 cup) pitted dates

2 eggs

1 cup sugar

1 cup (about 100g) chopped walnuts

1 cup boiling water

1 Tbsp butter (I use Crisco)

1 tsp baking soda

1 1/2 cup flour

FRUIT MUFFINS

Elisheva Cohen

Preheat oven to 225C (425F).

Muffins are easy to make. Put all the ingredients in a bowl and mix until there is a smooth batter. Be careful not to over mix. Bake in muffin tins for 25 minutes.

INGREDIENTS

1 1/2 cups whole-wheat flour

1 cup oats

2 tsp baking powder

1 egg

1 cup yogurt or milk

1/2 tsp cinnamon

1 apple, finely diced, with peel

1/2 cup berries or strawberries, fresh or frozen

1/3 cup brown sugar or honey

1/3 cup oil

GRANDMA LOIS'S FRUIT TORTE

Anonymous

Preheat oven to 180C (350F).

Mix oil and sugar. Add flour, baking powder, eggs, and vanilla. Pour into pan and cover with seasonal fruit: apples, peaches etc. Drizzle a little lemon juice, sugar, and cinnamon over the fruit. Bake for 45 minutes. Serve hot.

CAKE

1/2 cup oil
2/3 cup sugar
1 cup flour
1 tsp baking powder
1 tsp vanilla essence
2 eggs

FILLING

Seasonal fruit
Sugar, to taste
Lemon juice, to taste
Cinnamon, to taste

PEACH CAKE

Fran Ackerman

Preheat oven to 190C (375F).

Combine 5 Tbsp of sugar, fruit, and cinnamon. Set aside. In a separate bowl, combine dry ingredients (sugar, flour, baking powder, and salt) and mix. Add remaining ingredients and mix. Drain liquid from fruit mixture. Grease a 9x13 pan. Layer batter and fruit, starting and ending with batter (maximum two layers). Bake for 70 minutes. Check after 45 minutes and, if cake is brown, cover it. Variation: Substitute apples for peaches and use 5 tsp of cinnamon.

INGREDIENTS

3 cups peaches, sliced
3 tsp cinnamon
2 cups plus 5 Tbsp sugar
3 cups flour
3 tsp baking powder
1 tsp salt
1 cup oil
4 eggs
1/4 cup orange juice
1 tsp vanilla

INGREDIENTS

6 eggs

1 cup sugar

1 2/3 cup honey

1 1/4 cup oil

1 cup strong instant coffee

1 cup ginger ale

2 Tbsp baking powder

6 cups flour

1 tsp salt

1/2 tsp cinnamon

2 tsp baking soda

HONEY CAKE

Tzippy Gutman

Preheat oven to 180C (350F).

Beat eggs well. Add sugar, honey, and oil, and mix. Mix coffee with ginger ale. Add this liquid mixture alternately with flour mixture to the beaten eggs. Pour into lightly greased tube or loaf pan. Bake for 50 minutes, or test center.

INGREDIENTS

2 cups sugar

1 cup oil

4 eggs

1 cup water or juice

3 cups flour

Pinch of salt

2 heaping tsp baking powder

2 tsp vanilla essence

3 Tbsp cocoa

QUICK MARBLE CAKE

Ronit Hudak | Kibbutz Tirat Zvi

Beit She'an Valley

This is one of the easiest and tastiest cakes around, suitable for entertaining or any Chag. The page in my recipe book is covered with drips of batter proving how often I make it!

Preheat oven to 180C (350F).

Mix oil and sugar. Add eggs one at a time. Add the water alternatively with the flour, salt, baking powder, and vanilla essence. Pour 3/4 of the mixture into a greased oblong baking dish. Add the cocoa to the remaining mixture and mix well. Pour the brown mixture on top of the white mixture and "cut" the mixture several times with a knife. Do not stir! Bake for about 50 minutes.

BASIC SPONGE CAKE

Orit Ben-Eliyahu

Preheat oven to 180C (350F).

Whip egg whites until stiff and gradually add 3/4 cup sugar. Put aside. In a separate bowl beat egg yolks, 1/4 cup remaining sugar, oil, juice (or water), baking powder, flour and lemon peel. Gently fold egg white mixture into batter. Bake 45 minutes.

INGREDIENTS

4 eggs, separated

1 cup sugar

1/4 cup oil

1 cup juice or water

1 package baking powder

1 1/2 cups flour

lemon peel

optional: chocolate chips/nuts/dried fruit/coconut

WONDER POT CAKE

Nitsan, Re'ut, Tomer and Ariel Malchi

When our mother was little, Grandma Yocheved didn't have an oven. She would bake cakes in a special pot – a wonder pot on the stovetop. This remained our favorite cake even after she got an oven. It is simple and easy to make. We reached a family record when we joined forces and prepared it in four minutes.

Beat the egg whites while slowly adding sugar until stiff. Add the flour with baking powder alternately with the liquids. Coconut, cinnamon, and nutmeg may be added for flavor. Bake 45 minutes on a medium flame.

INGREDIENTS

4 eggs, separated

1 1/2 cups sugar

2 cups whole-wheat flour

3/4 cup orange juice

baking powder

coconut, cinnamon, nutmeg optional

DOUGH

8 cups less 2 Tbsp flour

1/3 cup sugar

50g fresh yeast/ "Shimrit" or 2 Tbsp dry active yeast

pinch of salt

1 1/4 cups water

3 eggs

400g (2 cups) margarine

FILLING

1/2 cup flour, for rolling dough

100g (1/2 cup) melted margarine

1 cup sugar

1/3 cup cocoa

1 egg yolk, beaten

GRANDMA TOVAH'S YEAST CAKE

Polak Family | Hungary

Preheat oven to 180C (350F).

Mix all dry ingredients. Add water, eggs, and margarine. Knead until well blended. Set dough aside to rise, for at least 1 hour. Divide dough into six. Roll out each ball thinly and generously brush with margarine. Blend sugar and cocoa and sprinkle on rolled out dough, make sure to leave borders clean. Roll lengthwise into a strip and seal ends. Use a knife to make 5 slashes on top of each strip and set aside to rise for 1 additional hour. Brush with egg yolk and bake for 35 minutes.

INGREDIENTS

1 cup cocoa

1 1/4 cup margarine

2 cups sugar

4 eggs

1 cup flour

1 tsp vanilla

1/2 tsp salt

150g (5 oz) chocolate chips

SERIOUSLY FUDGIE BROWNIES

Allegra Cohen

Preheat oven to180C (350F).

Cream sugar and eggs. Add margarine and cocoa. Add in the flour, salt, and vanilla. Mix. Fold in the chocolate chips. Bake for approximately 20-25 minutes in a 9x13 inch pan. Do not overbake. Brownies should be moist.

PEANUT BUTTER SQUARES

Shoshi Isaacs

Preheat oven to 180C (350F).

Mix together the egg, brown sugar, margarine, and vanilla for 5 minutes. When mixed well, add the flour. Bake in the oven for 15 minutes. Remove from oven and spread the peanut butter over. Sprinkle the chocolate chips on the peanut butter, and place in oven for 2 minutes. Remove from oven and spread the chocolate chips using a spatula.

INGREDIENTS

1 egg

1 cup brown sugar

1 cup margarine

1 tsp vanilla essence (extract)

2 cups flour

2 heaping Tbsp peanut butter

1 1/2 cups chocolate chips

PEANUT BUTTER RICE SQUARES

Ellen Cohl

Combine sugar and syrup. Bring to a boil, stirring constantly. Remove from heat. Add peanut butter and mix. Add Rice Krispies. Mix well. Pour into an 8-inch square pan. Let cool and harden. Cut into squares.

INGREDIENTS

1/2 cup sugar

1/2 cup dark karo syrup

3/4 cup peanut butter

2 1/2 cups Rice Krispies

TOFFEE SQUARES

Barbara Lang

INGREDIENTS

- 1 cup brown sugar
- 1 cup margarine
- 1 egg
- 1 tsp vanilla
- 2 cups flour
- 1 cup chocolate chips

Preheat oven to 180C (350F).

Cream sugar, margarine, egg, and vanilla. Add flour and beat until mixed. Bake in a 9x13 inch pan for 15 minutes. Remove the pan from the oven and sprinkle the chocolate chips on top. Return pan to oven for two minutes. Spread out the chocolate chips. Cut while still warm.

CHOCOLATE CHIP AND OATMEAL COOKIES

Avital and Yonatan Lisker

INGREDIENTS

- 1 cup margarine
- 2 cups brown sugar
- 4 eggs
- 1/2 cup orange juice
- grated orange rind
- salt
- 3 cups flour
- 2 tsp baking soda
- 2 1/2 cups oats
- 1 1/2 cups chocolate chips
- 1 1/2 cups raisins
- 1 1/2 cups walnuts

Preheat oven to 180C (350F).

Combine margarine and sugar. Add the eggs, orange juice, and the rest of the ingredients, and mix. Drop a teaspoonful at a time onto a baking sheet. Bake for 8-10 minutes.

BUBBY YETTA'S HAMENTASHEN

Ari and Michal Schlakman (Bubby Yetta's great-grandchildren)

Preheat oven to 180C (350F).

Mix together filling ingredients and set aside. Grate the skin of the orange. Squeeze juice from the orange. Beat orange juice together with eggs, sugar, oil, and grated peel of orange. Mix in baking powder and 2 cups of flour. Slowly add in more flour until the dough comes away from the sides of the bowl easily, and can roll and stretch. Roll dough out on floured board to about 1 cm (1/4 inch) thick. Cut dough with overturned glass of desired size and put teaspoon of filling in center. Fold sides in and pinch into triangle shape. Bake on greased cookie sheets for 15-20 minutes or until light brown. Once out of the oven and warm, brush with a little honey. Eat gezunteheit!

DOUGH
2-4 cups flour
2 eggs
1/2 cup oil
1/2 cup sugar
1 medium orange
2 tsp baking powder

FILLING
450g (16 oz) fruit jelly
1/2 cup raisins
drizzle of honey
1/2 cup chopped nuts

SPLIT SECOND COOKIES

Michelle Gordetzer

Preheat oven to 180C (350F).

Combine the dry ingredients. Mix in margarine, vanilla, and egg. Roll the dough into long strips. With your fingers, make an indentation down the length of the dough. Fill the indentation with jelly. Bake for 15-18 minutes. Let cool a bit, but cut into strips to make cookies while the dough is still warm.

INGREDIENTS
2 cups flour
1/2 tsp baking powder
2/3 cup sugar
150g (3/4 cup) margarine
1 unbeaten egg
2 tsp vanilla

SUGAR COOKIES

Naomi Schwartz

Preheat oven to 190C (400F).

Cream butter, oil, eggs, and sugars. Add flour, salt, baking soda, and vanilla. Mix until well blended. Refrigerate for at least one hour. Roll out dough on floured surface. Shape with cookie cutters and bake for approximately 8-10 minutes until golden brown.

INGREDIENTS

1 cup butter or margarine

1 cup oil

2 eggs

1 cup powdered sugar

1 cup sugar

4 cups and 4 Tbsp flour

1 tsp salt

1 tsp baking soda

1 tsp vanilla

APPLE CRISP

Plain & Fancy Catering | 02 654 0678

APPLE FILLING

Mix apples with other filling ingredients. Pour into a greased 9x13 inch pyrex dish.

TOPPING

Preheat oven to 180C (350F).

Crumble the cold margarine with the rest of the topping ingredients. Sprinkle over apple mixture. Bake about 40 minutes.

APPLE FILLING

16 apples, peeled & cut

2 Tbsp lemon juice

1/2 - 1 cup sugar

1 tsp cinnamon

TOPPING

100g (1/2 cup) margarine, cold

1 cup brown sugar

1 cup flour

APPLE CRUMBLE

Sara Weinstein

This can be made Kosher for Pesach! Just substitute the flour with Pesach cake meal or fine matzo meal.

FILLING

Core apples and cut into small pieces, you do not need to peel them. Mix with the other ingredients. Place in a 9 x 13 inch pan. Dot with margarine.

CRUMBLE

Preheat oven to 180C (350F).

Melt margarine, add flour, and brown sugar. Mix with fork, then mix with fingers until it is crumbly. Pour crumble on top of the apple mixture. Bake until crumble turns golden and juice starts to come out of the apples.

FILLING

6 - 8 cups apples or pears and apples, or peaches and apples, or just peaches

1 tsp vanilla sugar

2 Tbsp brown sugar

1/4 tsp cinnamon

2 Tbsp flour

margarine

CRUMBLE

100g (1/2 cup) margarine

1 cup flour

1 cup brown sugar

ORANGES IN RED WINE

Aliza Beinhaker

Dissolve sugar in the water and wine. Boil until it turns into a syrup. Pour over the oranges. Refrigerate and serve cool.

INGREDIENTS

6 oranges, peeled and sliced in circles

3/4 cup sugar

1 cup water

1 cup dry red wine

cinnamon to taste

lemon juice

POMEGRANATE JELLO DESSERT

Akiva Jacobs

INGREDIENTS

2 packages of strawberry or rasberry jello, or one of each

seeds of 1 large pomegranate

plastic mold, greased

Prepare the jello as directed on the package. Pour the jello into the greased mold, and then pour the pomegranate seeds on top. Put it in the refridgerator for at least 3 hours before serving.

COFFEE AND MERINGUE ICE CREAM

Noga Tur-Paz

INGREDIENTS

1 container Rich's whipping cream

1 Tbsp instant coffee

5 to 6 meringue cookies or chocolate sandwich cookies, crumbled

Whip cream and coffee. Stir in cookies. Freeze in freezer.

MOCHA CHIP MERINGUES

Zavi Apfelbaum

From my mom, Susie Srebro

Preheat oven to 180C (350F).

Beat egg whites stiff while slowly adding sugar. Drizzle in a bit of lemon juice. Once egg white is stiff, carefully incorporate the coffee and cocoa. Fold in nuts and chocolate. I like to use a sheet of foil on the baking pan. Drop spoonfuls on pan, leaving a bit of space between each cookie. Bake on upper rack for about 25 minutes (you have to experiment with your oven).

INGREDIENTS

2 egg whites

3/4 cup sugar

bit of lemon juice

1 Tbsp coffee powder

1 Tbsp cocoa powder

3/4 cup chopped walnuts

3/4 cup chocolate chips

CHOCOLATE SACK

Ettie Davies

Preheat oven to 220C (425F).

Thaw the pastry. On a lightly floured surface, roll pastry to a 35cm (14 inch) square. In the center of the square, place the chocolate, nuts if you are using them, and the margarine. Sprinkle with liquor. Pull the pastry edges together, then twist and turn to make a nice "flower." Place on an ungreased baking sheet and bake 20 minutes. Let stand 10 minutes. Sprinkle with confection sugar.

INGREDIENTS

1 sheet frozen puff pastry dough

1 package chocolate chips

1 Tbsp Kahlua or coffee liqueur

1/3 cup chopped nuts, (optional)

30g (2 Tbsp) margarine

confectionary sugar

CLAFOUTIS

Estie Seville

A traditional French dish from the Limousine Region.

Preheat oven to 190C (375F).

Mix flour and sugar. Whip the cream and add eggs one at a time until well blended. Gently stir in fruit. Grease deep Pyrex dish and pour in batter. Bake approximately 15 minutes, increase temperature to 220C (425F) and bake an additional 1/2 hour. Check that the batter is baked through and don't worry if the top appears slightly burned.

INGREDIENTS

6 Tbsp flour

6 Tbsp sugar

1 container sweet heavy cream

5 eggs

6 apples, thinly sliced or cherries (canned or frozen) or any other fruit

FROZEN CHOCOLATE MOUSSE PIE

Hillary Morris Catering | 02 993 2043 | 050 555 4045

MOUSSE

Preheat oven to 190C (375F).

Melt the chocolate with 6 Tbsp chocolate liqueur. Beat the yolks with 4 Tbsp chocolate liqueur. Add the melted chocolate to the yolks. Beat the egg whites with the cream of tartar. Set aside. Beat the Rich's Whip. Fold the whip into the melted chocolate. Then combine the chocolate mixture with the whites.

CRUST

Take off 1/3 of the mousse mixture and mix in 5 Tbsp flour. Mix well. Put into a 10 inch spring form pan. Bake for 15 minutes. Cool. Add mousse and freeze.

MOUSSE

360g (12 oz) semi sweet chocolate

10 Tbsp chocolate liqueur, divided

6 eggs, separated

1/2 tsp cream of tartar

1 container Rich's Whip

CRUST

5 Tbsp flour

DRY MEASUREMENT EQUIVALENTS

1/4 lb = 125g
1/2 lb = 250g
1 lb = 500g
2 lbs = 1kg
3 lbs = 1.5kg
4 lbs = 2kg
5 lbs = 2.5kg

LIQUID MEASUREMENT EQUIVALENTS

1/4 tsp = 1.5ml
1/2 tsp = 3ml
1 tsp = 5ml
1 Tbsp = 15ml
1/3 cup = 80ml
1/2 cup = 125ml
3/4 cup = 200ml
1 cup = 250ml

OVEN TEMPERATURE EQUIVALENTS

200F = 100C
250F = 120C
275F = 140C
300F = 160C
325F = 170C
350F = 180C
375F = 190C
400F = 200C
425F = 220C
450F = 230C
475F = 240C
500F = 260C
525F = 270C
550F = 280C

We would like to thank all of those people and restaurants who contributed their delicious recipes for this cookbook. We are grateful to everyone who volunteered time and energy to make this cookbook a success.

Special thanks to Shellie Davis, Elisheva Hershler, and Amy Schlakman whose hard work and devotion made this book a reality. Thanks to Shari Greenspan for her professional editing skills. Thanks to Zahava Bogner who donated her time and professional expertise for the graphic design and layout of this cookbook. Thanks to Cheli Wolfstahl who donated her professional design skills in the design and layout of the Hebrew version of the book. Thanks to David Cohen and Rebecca Kowalsky for their professional photography of the children and our school. Thanks to Sima Navon who did an amazing job fund-raising for this cookbook.

Marilyn Adler	*Zohara Heimann*
Dena Bailey	*Sarit Herbst*
Elaine Beychok	*Elisheva Hershler*
Zahava Bogner	*Rebecca Kowalsky*
David Cohen	*Barbara Lang*
Tanya Cohen	*Menachem Levi*
Ettie Davies	*David Marcus*
Eric Davis	*Sima Navon*
Shellie Davis	*Miriam Ohayon*
Rachel Epstein	*Dena Pickholz*
Sima Freedman	*Amy Schlakman*
Naomi Freudenberger	*Anat Stein*
Suzie Friedman	*Hazel Vahav*
Shari Greenspan	

We would also like to thank Tzvi Mauer of *Urim Publications* for his important role in the printing and publishing of this cookbook.

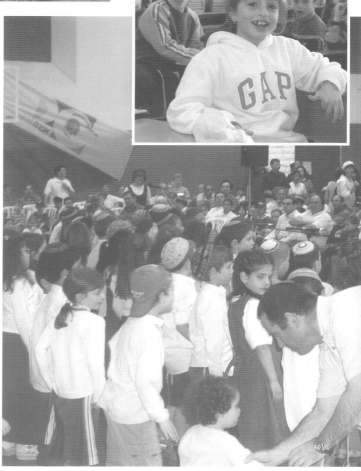